Robert Delaunay   Light and Color

The Tower with Curtains 1910

Gustav Vriesen   Max Imdahl

Robert Delaunay: Light and Color

Harry N. Abrams, Inc. *Publishers* New York

Translated from German by Maria Pelikan

Library of Congress Catalog Card Number: 69-17034

Printed and bound in West Germany

Contents

I Robert Delaunay La Lumière

Été 1912 ~~...~~

— La Lumière —

l'Impressionnisme; c'est la naissance de la Lumière en peinture

La lumière nous vient par la sensibilité.

Sans la sensibilité visuelle aucune lumière aucun mouvement

La lumière dans la Nature crée le mouvement des couleurs

Le mouvement est donné par les rapports les mesures impaires

· des contrastes des couleurs entre elles et qui constitue la Réalité

Cette réalité est douée de la Profondeur (nous voyons jusqu'aux étoiles)

et devient alors la Simultanéité rythmique

La simultanéité c'est dans la lumière c'est l'harmonie le rythme des couleurs

qui crée la Vision des Hommes

La Vision humaine est douée de la plus grande Réalité puisqu'elle

nous vient directement de la contemplation de l'Univers

l'Œil est notre sens le plus élevé celui qui communique le plus étroite-

ment avec notre cerveau la conscience l'idée du mouvement vital du

monde et son mouvement est simultanéité.

Notre compréhension est corrélative à notre perception ~~il faut~~

cherchons à Voir

La perception auditive ne suffit pas pour notre connaissance

de l'Univers elle n'a pas de profondeur

Son mouvement est successif c'est une sorte de mécanisme sa loi

est le temps des horloges mécaniques qui comme elle n'a aucune

relation avec notre perception du mouvement visuel dans l'Univers

C'est la parité des choses de la géométrie

Sa qualité se rapproche de l'Objet conçu géométriquement ·

l'Objet n'est pas doué de Vie de mouvement

Quand il est Simulacre du mouvement il devient Successif

dynamique

Sa plus grande limite est d'un ordre pratique Véhicule

Le chemin de fer est l'image de ce Successif qui se rapproche

des parallèles la parité du Rail

Ainsi de l'Architecture la Sculpture

Le plus grand objet de la Terre est assujetti à ces mêmes lois

Il devient... simulacre de la hauteur

2   La Tour Eiffel

de la largeur

les Villes

Longueur

Rails

l'Art dans la Nature est rythmique   et a horreur de la contrainte

Si l'Art s'apparente à l'Objet il devient descriptif littéraire

divisioniste littéraire

Il s'abaisse vers des moyens d'expression imparfaits il se condamne de

lui-même il est sa propre négation il ne se dégage pas de

l'Art d'imitation

Si de même il représente les relations visuelles d'un objet ou

des objets entre eux sans que la lumière joue le rôle

d'ordonnance de la représentation

Il est conventionnel il n'arrive pas à la pureté plastique

c'est une infirmité il est la négation de la vie le sublime

de l'Art de la peinture

Pour que l'Art atteigne la limite de sublimité il faut

qu'il se rapproche de notre Vision harmonique la clarté

La Clarté sera couleur, proportion ces proportions sont

composées de diverses mesures simultanées dans une action

Cette action doit être l'harmonie représentative le mouvement

Synchrome qui est la seule réalité

Cette action Synchromique sera donc le sujet qui est

l'harmonie représentative

R. Delaunay

La Lumière[1]

L'Impressionnisme, c'est la naissance de la *Lumière* en peinture.

La lumière nous vient par la sensibilité.

Sans la sensibilité visuelle, aucune lumière, aucun mouvement.

La lumière dans la Nature crée le mouvement des couleurs.

Le mouvement est donné par les rapports *des mesures impaires*, des contrastes des couleurs entre elles et qui constitue *la Réalité*.

Cette réalité est douée de la *Profondeur* (nous voyons jusqu'aux étoiles), et devient alors la *Simultanéité rythmique*.

La simultanéité dans la lumière, c'est *l'harmonie, le rythme des couleurs* qui crée la *Vision des Hommes*.

La vision humaine est douée de la plus grande Réalité puisqu'elle nous vient directement de la contemplation de l'Univers.

L'Oeil est notre sens le plus élevé, celui qui communique le plus étroitement avec notre *cerveau, la conscience*. L'idée du mouvement vital du *monde, et son mouvement est simultanéité*.

Notre compréhension est *corrélative* à notre *perception*. *Cherchons à voir.*

La perception auditive ne suffit pas pour notre connaissance de l'Univers; elle n'a pas *de profondeur*.[2]

Son mouvement est *successif*, c'est une sorte de mécanisme; *sa loi* est *le temps* des horloges *mécaniques* qui, comme elles, n'a aucune relation avec notre perception *du mouvement visuel dans l'Univers*.

C'est la parité des choses de la géométrie.

Sa qualité le rapproche de *l'Objet conçu géométriquement*.

L'Objet n'est pas doué de *vie, de mouvement*.

Quand il est *simulacre du mouvement*, il devient *successif, dynamique*.

Sa plus grande limite est d'un *ordre pratique*. *Véhicules*.

Le chemin de fer est *l'image* de ce successif qui se rapproche *des parallèles: la parité du Rail*.

Ainsi de l'Architecture, la Sculpture.

Le plus grand objet de la Terre est assujetti à ces mêmes lois.

Il deviendra simulacre de la hauteur:

La Tour Eiffel;

de la largeur:

Les Villes;

longueur:

Rails.

L'Art dans la *Nature est rythmique et a horreur de la contrainte*.

Si l'Art s'apparente *à l'Objet*, il devient *descriptif, divisionniste, littéraire*.

Il se rabaisse vers des *moyens d'expression* imparfaits, il se condamne de lui-même, il est sa propre négation, *il ne se dégage pas de l'Art d'imitation*.

Si de même il représente *les relations visuelles* d'un objet ou *des objets entre eux* sans que la *lumière joue le rôle d'ordonnance de la représentation*,

il est conventionnel, il n'arrive pas à *la pureté plastique;* c'est une *infirmité;* il est la négation de la vie, *la sublimité de l'Art de la peinture*.

Pour que l'Art atteigne la limite de sublimité, il faut qu'il se rapproche de notre *Vision harmonique: la clarté*.

La clarté sera couleur, proportion; ces proportions sont composées de diverses mesures simultanées dans une action.

Cette action doit être l'harmonie représentative, *le mouvement synchrome (simultanéité) de la lumière*, qui est la *seule réalité*.

Cette action synchromique sera donc le Sujet qui est l'harmonie représentative.

Robert Delaunay

Light[3]

Impressionism is the birth of *Light* in painting.

Light reaches us through our perception.

Without visual perception, no light, no movement.

Light in Nature creates movement of colors.

The movement is provided by the relationships *of uneven measures*, of color contrasts among themselves and [it] constitutes *Reality*.

This reality is endowed with *Depth* (we see as far as the stars), and thus becomes *rhythmic Simultaneity*.

Simultaneity in light is *the harmony, the rhythm of colors* which creates *Men's Sight*.

Human sight is endowed with the greatest Reality since it comes to us directly from contemplation of the Universe.

The Eye is our highest sense, the one that communicates most closely with our *brain, our consciousness*, the idea of the vital movement of the *world*, and *its movement is simultaneity*.

Our comprehension is *correlative* with our *perception. Let us try to see.*

Auditory perception does not suffice for our knowledge of the Universe; it has no *depth*.[4]

Its movement is *successive*, it is a kind of mechanism; *its principle* is *the time* of *mechanical* clocks which, like them, has no relation to our perception *of visual movement in the Universe.*

This is the evenness of things in geometry.

Its character makes it resemble *the Object conceived geometrically.*

The *Object* is not endowed with *Life, with movement.*

When it has the *appearance of movement*, it becomes *successive, dynamic.*

Its greatest limitation is of a *practical order. Vehicles.*

The railroad is *the image* of this successiveness which resembles *parallels: the evenness of Track.*

So with Architecture, Sculpture.

The mightiest object on Earth is subject to these same laws.

It will become the appearance of height:

The Eiffel Tower;

of breadth:

Cities;

length:

Tracks.

Art in *Nature is rhythmic and abhors constraint.*

If art is attached *to the Object*, it becomes *descriptive, divisive, literary.*

It lowers itself to imperfect *means of expression*, it condemns itself of its own accord, it is its own negation, *it does not break free of imitative Art.*

If likewise it represents *the visual relationships* of an object or *between objects* without *light playing the role of governing the representation.*

It is conventional, it does not achieve *plastic purity;* it is a *weakness;* it is the negation of life, *of the sublimity of the Art of painting.*

For Art to reach the limits of sublimity, it must approach our *harmonic Vision: clarity.*

Clarity will be color, proportions; these proportions are composed of various simultaneous measures within an action.

This action must be representative harmony, *the synchromatic movement (simultaneity) of light*, which is the *only reality.*

This synchromatic action will then be the Subject which is the representative harmony.

Robert Delaunay

1 Delaunay's text, as shown in facsimile on the preceding pages, is printed in Robert Delaunay, *Du Cubisme à l'Art abstrait*, ed. by Pierre Francastel, Paris, 1957, pp. 146ff. The facsimile was taken from the catalog of the Robert Delaunay exhibition, Kunsthalle, Bern, 1951, pp. 4 ff.

2 Variant: "puisqu'elle ne reste pas dans la durée."

3 Translation of the facsimile text. The punctuation of the edition by Francastel has been disregarded.

4 Variant: "for it has no duration."

R. DELAUNAY   LA BARAQUE DES POÈTES

La Baraque des Poètes 1922

1910
Delaunay "La Tour"

The Tower 1910

II Gustav Vriesen

Robert Delaunay's Life and Work
from the Beginning to Orphism

1885–1909

Robert Delaunay was born toward the end of the nineteenth century into a world that has been vividly described by Marcel Proust – a vanished world in which the French aristocracy had just begun to mingle with and become dissolved within a rising bourgeoisie.

Both his parents belonged to the French nobility of the young Third Republic. By choice and tradition, they led an extremely fashionable life; their house was elegant to the point of sumptuousness. Their way of life had enormous style, but it was also pretentious, egotistical, frivolous. People simply never asked whether they could actually afford to live in this rich, resplendent style. They chose to live like kings, and squandered their financial inheritance.

Delaunay's father, Georges, came from a noble family in Picardy, and his grandfather had been postmaster general under Napoleon III, a position of social prestige. We are told that Georges was a spoiled, elegant worldling who owned "a hundred hats and boots."

Robert's mother, the Countess Berthe-Félicie de Rose, came from an aristocratic family whose name is said to go back to the time of the Crusades. Robert-Victor-Félix Delaunay, an only child, was born on the Rue de Chaillot in Paris on April 12, 1885. His parents were divorced a few years later. Robert stayed with his mother. He had barely known his father before the divorce and never saw him again.

A photograph taken just before the turn of the century (see p. 89) casts a ghostly light on that milieu of exquisite artificiality in which his mother lived. "La belle Mademoiselle de Rose," as Berthe Delaunay was called in her youth, is posing in a white negligee in the dimly lit dressing room of her large, richly appointed apartment on the Avenue d'Alma. Her arm is raised in a prettily futile gesture toward her intricate curly coiffure. Her face is self-consciously beautiful and somewhat blasé. The frozen pose, the big palm tree, the highlights gleaming on the expensive furniture, the opulent cushions, flowers, vases, lamps, and candlesticks – all contribute to the theatricality of the scene, which brings to mind the young Eleonora Duse.

Berthe Delaunay was no ordinary woman. She had taste and a natural affinity for the arts. It was taken for granted that she would attend every important event in the world of art. She herself painted in the Neoimpressionist manner and did flower embroideries for fashion designers. She brought an open mind and sound judgment to all forms of art. Later, she was the only one in the family who understood and defended Robert's work. Driven by a great need for attention and gifted with a knack for becoming the center of any group, she gave parties at her studios that brought the entire elite of Paris together. She sought and enjoyed the company of the new painters and poets whom she met through her son. Guillaume Apollinaire was a frequent guest at her later apartment, near Saint-Germain-des-Prés, with its marvelous signed Empire pieces. Henri Rousseau's famous painting *The Snake Charmer* hung in the dining room.

For the first few years after her divorce, Berthe Delaunay, restless and ever hungry for new experiences, traveled a great deal. For months on end she visited faraway places: Russia, Africa, India.

Though she was very fond of her son, she was much too enterprising, too fashionable and egocentric, and too prone to make scenes to be a good mother to him. The patience and day-to-day steadiness needed to raise a child were simply not in her nature. Besides, she was almost always off on a trip somewhere. She relegated the care of Robert to her older sister Marie and to Marie's husband, Charles Damour. Thus Robert came to spend a large part of his childhood at his uncle's country place, La Ronchère, near Bourges. It was a large estate with a palatial mansion in the middle of a great park that gradually blended into the surrounding countryside. Life was calm and secure there. Aunt Marie, quite different from her sister, was happily married, unpretentious; an affectionate, kindly woman, she played mother to the young Robert. Her husband took the part of a father and guardian upon himself. He was an amateur painter who had once studied under Fernand Cormon. His paintings were sensitive but definitely academic. Charles Damour was a traditionalist in his way of life and in his paintings. This was to lead to violent disagreements between him and his modernist, revolutionary nephew in later years.

At La Ronchère (see fig. 1, p. 91), Robert had ample time and opportunity to wander about outdoors and observe flowers, plants, and animals for hours on end. Direct contact with nature and with the country and country people was congenial to him. His intuitive understanding of natural processes and his gentle affection for all living things developed at that time. They remained two of his most important character traits. In 1938, he still enjoyed telling his friends how he had crept close to a singing lark as a boy, and how farmers and woodcutters had taught him about the way a tree grows and how to tell its age. He was at home in nature.

The freedom he enjoyed at La Ronchère agreed with him. This always became especially apparent when his mother returned from one of her trips and took him back to Paris, where, dressed to the teeth, he would be taken for walks along the Champs-Élysées. Even as a little boy, he abhorred the fashionable life and resisted it with every means at his command. Delaunay was always difficult, but the obstinacy with which he fought his mother's attempts at educating him was certainly based on his deep, intuitive dislike of an unnatural, artificial world. This aversion never left him.

Delaunay's adult personality clearly showed the traces of both these diametrically opposite environments of his youth. A born Parisian, lively, critical, open-minded, Delaunay appeared to be a man of the world. He was tall, blond, and good-looking. He had his mother's large, light eyes. His natural elegance betrayed his background, his noble ancestry. There is no doubt that Robert Delaunay, whether he liked it or not, was decisively marked by his origins. He was his parents' son – in his great self-esteem, in his egotism, and in the naïveté with which he took his own importance for granted. All his life he wanted to be the center of attention wherever he went. But he also had a lifelong aversion to the fashionable rites of social life, frivolous jokes, and empty conversation. This man who radiated such arrogant self–assurance also had a distinct penchant toward the simple and unaffected. He liked the company of simple people and could talk with them for hours in a perfectly natural way without a grain of condescension. His apartment in town was filled with exquisite plants which he observed and tended lovingly. F. Gilles de la Tourette, Delaunay's first biographer, who saw him in his Paris studio on the Rue Saint-Simon a few years before the artist's death, describes the affectionate way Delaunay would expertly and tenderly touch a leaf and help it get free to turn toward the light. He was fascinated not only by the splendor of blossoms but by the process of growth itself, the unfolding of the living plant.

Robert went to school first in Paris, and later to the boarding school of Sainte-Marie in Bourges. Like many people who are destined to concentrate all their vital and creative energy on a single field and to accomplish great things in it, he was a poor student. Sleepy, lazy, and uninterested, he woke up only for the subjects that appealed to his own developing spirit: drawing and natural history. "That was all I was interested in," he confessed later. The adult Delaunay's letters show a sovereign unconcern for the rules of spelling – just as, in his boyhood, he had alternated between apathy and antagonism toward every kind of school- and book-learning. Later he was to apply the epithet *scholastic* to everything that seemed dry, schoolmasterish, and abstract to him, filling him with immediate, instinctive dislike. It is understandable that his teachers were not fond of him: his incorrigible laziness got him expelled from one school after another. He finally landed at the Lycée Michelet at Vanves, where he stayed until he was seventeen. At this time, he very firmly told his uncle that he wanted to be a painter. His family seems to have resigned itself to the idea that his academic training had come to an end.

In 1902, Robert was apprenticed to the Rosin Decorative Studio in Belleville, which produced theatrical backdrops. He spent two years there. The only memento of that period is a photograph of Delaunay at the age of

In Paris in 1905, Delaunay painted his first self-portrait, *Self-Portrait with Japanese Print* (fig. 37). This unfinished picture is important because of its position in time and also because it shows the pretentious self-assurance of the twenty-year-old. It is interesting to compare this picture with the photograph (p. 89), which shows the head in almost exactly the same pose in the opposite direction. In the painting, Delaunay seems much older than he actually was at the time. No doubt he took himself very seriously and paid careful attention to the interpretation of his spiritual self. His sense of large-looking shapes – the head is all depth and expression – is here combined with a self-stylization that emphasizes the deep furrows around the eyes, nose, and mouth, the thick shock of hair, the workingman's neckerchief; a general proletarian effect is aimed for. And this is further strengthened by the crude application of paint. The face is greenish yellow, the hair purple. Despite the self-contained seriousness of the face, the whole is not quite free from pathos. One feels the inner protest against the elegance of his family, against this world whose false brilliance may well have signaled the beginning of decay.

We know very little about the circumstances in which Delaunay lived at that time. According to his friend Philippe Soupault, he lived in Pleine Monceau on the Rue Legendre, among "gray streets without shops, without cries, without pedestrians; streets that do not come to life until dark."[1] But it seems that he was not especially happy in those humble surroundings.

The fall of 1905 brought a change in Delaunay's painting. Until then he had used color instinctively; now his attention was drawn to the methods of Neoimpressionism. Though Delaunay's Neoimpressionist phase lasted only two years, it was of paramount importance for his entire work.

Neoimpressionism was twenty years old and its theory fully developed when Delaunay came under the spell of this movement. Like certain aspects of Impressionism, Neoimpressionism was based on scientific findings about light and color that had appeared as early as 1839, in M. E. Chevreul's book *De la Loi du contraste simultané des couleurs (The Principles of Harmony and Contrast of Colors . . .).*[2] Georges Seurat had leaned on them when, in the 1880s, he began to systematize the Impressionist painters' often instinctive and empirical color effects by strictly separating color into its components and marking the various color values exactly with dots. In place of the usual mixture of pigments – which, when representing natural light effects on canvas, often retained its palpable and impure character – he separated light into its constituent color elements and placed them in such a way that the mixture took place in the viewer's eye as an "optical mixture."

By thus placing color values and light values on canvas in the way that light does in nature, Seurat believed that he was merely "improving" on the Impressionist technique. Actually, however, he achieved a liberation of color in the artistic consciousness, a process whose consequences were to lead far beyond the boundaries of Impressionism. The individual color value, which had been merely the result of analytical dissection, took on a new meaning in the Pointillist system; it became the building block, the starting point and basic element, of an entirely new, independent pictorial structure which developed its own autonomous laws, created a new relationship between depth and surface, and thus transcended the old illusionism.

Delaunay's pictures of 1905 to 1907 suggest that he got his first determining impressions from Henri-Edmond Cross (1856–1910), who belonged to Seurat's circle and who, along with Paul Signac, led the Neo-impressionist movement into the twentieth century. A Cross one-man show, arranged by the Galerie Druet in 1905, may have given the first impetus. Delaunay did not comprehend the special significance of Seurat until some years later, but it is possible that as early as 1905 he had seen Seurat's most important works, which were in the hands of Félix Fénéon, who later became the head of the Galerie Bernheim-Jeune.

For a young man living in Paris who was at home in the world of art, it was not hard to know and see what trends were becoming dominant and where the new centers were forming:

Paris at that time was simple and clear [wrote the art collector and author Wilhelm Uhde shortly after his arrival in Paris], not stuffed full of confusing things. One knew where to go if one wanted to see beautiful pictures. Durand-Ruel, Vollard, Bernheim-Jeune were on the Rue Laffitte, Paul Rosenberg and Hessel on the Avenue de l'Opéra, Druet on the Faubourg Saint-Honoré. Then there were three or four other, smaller galleries. That was all. The Impressionist painters predominated. After terrible financial crises, after years of vilification and derision, Durand-Ruel had carried the day with them. In his shop and in his apartment we saw them triumph. . . . Cézanne and Gauguin were in Vollard's shop on the Rue Laffitte, a few steps closer to the boulevards. On the next street, Bernheim-Jeune had a small gallery with charming pictures by Bonnard, Vuillard, and some by Signac and Cross. It was easy then to get an over-all view of what was happening in Paris in the world of painting. Inside of two hours, one could visit every gallery of modern painting; inside of three days, one could find out everything about the painters themselves. In the Salon d'Automne and in the Indépendants, the best painters of the period could be found, and artists of second and third rank could easily be remembered in the few rooms of those exhibitions.[3]

In his Neoimpressionistic pictures, Delaunay first came to terms with the problems which later filled all his artistic thought: light, color, structure. Although in these pictures things were still represented in the way an older generation was used to seeing them, they nevertheless bespoke a new consciousness, a new tension and freshness, next to which the older pictures seemed drab. The joy in the elementary life of color had been awakened. For the first time, the spirit of creative experiment could be felt at work.

The reason Delaunay admired and emulated Cross was undoubtedly the brilliance of his colors. Delaunay felt that Seurat's optical mixture of color was too diffuse and incorporeal. Like Cross, he now largely emancipated himself from nature in his use of color; he also emulated Cross's way of applying color in rather large, robust patches, but at the same time he went beyond his model and arranged these rectangular patches in parallel horizontal layers and in circles or spirals, so that a noticeably mosaic-like structure emerged. The "mosaic stones" of his color patches are so large that no optical mixture takes place in the viewer's eye. The pictures Delaunay painted in this manner – portraits, landscapes, still lifes – have a strongly experimental character. Occasionally, when he stuck too rigidly to his dogma, they border on the academic, as does for instance his *Portrait of Wilhelm Uhde* (fig. 41). Of the pictures which emphasize ornament and structure, *Young Girl* – also called *The Poet* – has the most finished pictorial appearance (fig. 40).

A remarkable picture in this group is the small *Landscape with Disc* (fig. 5), in which a setting sun is seen above a spacious river landscape. The aureole of light has been turned into a circular motif of solid contours; it thus seems an early, still unconscious anticipation of Delaunay's later discs and circular forms.

Alongside these pictures, in which Delaunay experimented with his new method and its possibilities, there are a few real masterpieces. These are pictures which combine the new technique freely with older experience but which, in their coloristic finesse and compactness, suggest some contact with Pierre Bonnard. The decisive thing in these pictures is the sovereign ease and freedom and seeming effortlessness with which Delaunay accomplished this synthesis. In quality, these pictures not only

far outstripped everything he had painted before; they were already masterpieces of their time.

The two portraits of Monsieur and Madame Carlier are among the earliest of this phase. Henri Carlier and his mother were distant relatives of Delaunay's; one feels the family closeness and human warmth in both pictures. They probably were painted in the Carliers' country house in Vaulx-de-Cernay.

In the *Portrait of Madame Carlier* (fig. 42), with its rich but muted palette, the lightly stippled, suggestive method of painting is balanced against the spatial effect of the bright silhouette with its decoratively drawn outline. The influence of the Nabis is unmistakable. The loose, fluffy technique corresponds with the soft elegance of the sitter's bent head; similarly, the personality of her son, Henri Carlier (fig. 43), is complemented by the close, energetically built-up brush strokes and by the strong, warm colors. The picture of the man calmly sitting and reading in his garden exudes the magic of a comfortable bourgeois afternoon. The straw hat, pushed back from the forehead and turned up in front, adds an Oriental touch and makes the sitter seem unobserved and carefree. The entire canvas is densely, richly ornamental. Its shimmering contrasts have a jewel-like effect. The dark green leaves in the background stand against a deep blue sky. Their color tints the yellow-white straw hat, the vividly pink face, and the light vest with greenish and bluish highlights that contrast strongly with the dark green and dark blue "mosaic stones" in his jacket and beard.

In 1905 and 1906, Delaunay saw a great deal of the painter Jean Metzinger (1883–1956). Their friendship was cemented by a common interest in Neoimpressionism. They may even have met before, in Brittany, and Metzinger may well have been the one who suggested that particular vacation spot. This is the first we learn of a friendship with another artist. Metzinger later became an important Cubist painter, and in 1912, together with Albert Gleizes, he published *Du "Cubisme,"* which stated the case for Cubism.

To judge by Metzinger's letters to Delaunay, the two artists communicated in a relaxed, bantering tone. They discussed the scientific color research of Chevreul and O. N. Rood, which was of fundamental importance for the theory of Neoimpressionism. The friends often painted together, too. Delaunay did three portraits of Metzinger, and there exists a portrait of Delaunay by Metzinger.

The most interesting of Delaunay's versions is the one known as *The Man with the Tulip* (fig. 4), dated May, 1906. If we compare this picture with the two Carlier portraits, we notice immediately how very much Delau-

The two men met through the Indépendants, where Rousseau had been showing his pictures every year since 1886. He would lug them there on a handcart, serenely unmoved by the fact that, year after year, a highly amused public made fun of them. And indeed, his pictures stood out strangely from their surroundings. To eyes that had only just become accustomed to Impressionism's sophisticated vision, Rousseau's pictures seemed the clumsy, naïvely comical efforts of a Sunday painter.

There was a small group, however, who regarded these pictures with growing love and attention. In it were many of the great names of the future: Delaunay, Léger, Pablo Picasso, Maurice de Vlaminck, Max Jacob, Guillaume Apollinaire. These then young men's reports and reminiscences on their encounters and talks with the sixty-two-year-old Rousseau show a mixture of admiration, amazement, and irony that throws some light on the puzzling and fascinating effect of his work and its peculiar approach to reality.

In 1911, one year after Rousseau's death, Delaunay began work on an essay about him: "Henri Rousseau, Le Douanier: His Life and His Work."[4] Here are some excerpts from the projected essay:

The name of Rousseau is intimately connected with that of the Indépendants during a period when the first living symptoms of the *new* in French art, and in art generally, began to appear.

Rousseau is the grandfather of the artistic revolution in modern art.

He lived very modestly on a small state pension of about 1,200 francs. He gave lessons in painting, singing, and violin at home, and he sold his pictures mostly to people with small incomes, people of his own social sphere. In this atmosphere of Paris and within his milieu, Rousseau thus created his anonymous work – one might say in deep secret communion with the folk art of all countries. But he also marked it with the personal signature of his strength and will, and with that purity of style which characterized all of his life and work.

This kind of art, which one finds in the suburbs, villages, and small towns – the naïve, direct expression of these craftsmen, these country-fair artists, barbers, and milkmen; this entire body of painting that has sprung from the very roots of the people – Rousseau was its genius, its priceless blossom.[5]

Delaunay often visited Rousseau on the Rue Perrel, and attended the musical evenings which the old man gave in his studio.

In his enthusiasm, Delaunay introduced Rousseau to his mother. She entertained him with stories about her travels in India. Le Douanier's powerful imagination immediately transformed what he heard into images: during the weeks that followed, he painted *The Snake Charmer* (1907), which Berthe bought. She also introduced Rousseau to Wilhelm Uhde, whose art collection, then just begun, was to become famous. Uhde wrote about *The Snake Charmer*, "She [Berthe Delaunay] took me to his studio where I saw, standing on its easel, the magnificent jungle picture *The Snake Charmer*, which was later owned by Doucet, who then left it to the Louvre. During my subsequent visits to the old Douanier, I saw him gradually complete the picture."[6]

Not long afterward, Uhde gave the first one-man show of Henri Rousseau's works in his small gallery on the Rue Notre-Dame-des-Champs.

With all his love and admiration for Rousseau, Delaunay was of course not at all influenced by the old man's work. In that respect, they were worlds apart. On the other hand, in 1907 Delaunay's profound and fateful dialogue with the work of Paul Cézanne (1839–1906) began.

Delaunay is said to have remarked later in life, "Just as all of us have sprung from Cézanne, so all the others will have to spring from us." By then, Delaunay was fully aware of his own historic position, and felt himself deeply rooted in the French tradition. In his writings, he frequently acknowledged his debt to Cézanne, whose total effect on his own work he could evaluate in retrospect. Earlier in his life, he probably saw only certain partial aspects of the Cézanne influence, notably when they happened to be important or to have some bearing on the situation of the moment.

The earliest pictures showing Cézanne's influence are two still lifes entitled *Vases and Objects* (see fig. 47), both dated 1907. Delaunay painted them in the little roof-top studio on the Quai du Louvre where he worked from 1906 to 1909. It was on the eighth floor of the house in which his mother briefly occupied an apartment; he kept the studio even after she moved to the Left Bank. The precious vases and dishes in the still lifes belonged to Berthe Delaunay.

There is a new simplicity in these pictures. A new feeling for the plain, objective existence of things has replaced the ornamental splendor of the Neoimpressionist still lifes. The objects stand tangibly in space. The dot-and-line manner of Neoimpressionism has been abandoned. Instead, the painting technique, surface treatment, and spatial sense and the somewhat slanting view in the smaller picture (fig. 47) unmistakably show the Cézanne influence. The dark green, blue-green, and blue of the vases and dishes harmonize quietly and

elegantly with the brown table and the purple hues of the background. The half-light in which the room is bathed unifies the whole picture and lends mysterious life to the shimmering surfaces. This quality of the costly and the intimate is a new tone in Delaunay's work, to which the small format contributes.

Having had his military service deferred for a year, Delaunay was drafted in the autumn of 1907 and assigned to the 45th Infantry Regiment in Laon. After six months of training, he was transferred to the reserves for health reasons and put to work as a librarian. The landscape painter Robert Lotiron, who served with him, remembers that his work in the library left Delaunay ample time to pursue his own interests: he painted sets for a play his company produced, and poked through the library, where he came across the German philosophers, Spinoza, and the poems of Jules Laforgue, which especially delighted him. He also painted a view (now lost) of the Cathedral of Laon with its characteristic silhouette. His conversations with Lotiron revolved around his experience of Cézanne.

Altogether, it seems that the time Delaunay served in the army was not wasted. On the contrary, working with books seemed to encounter an inner readiness in him. He now could more thoroughly pursue all those questions and ideas that had come up while he painted or talked with friends, questions that may have made him feel the gaps in his education. Great as his aversion for school-enforced learning had been, he was now wide awake and eagerly interested in everything which had some bearing on his own ideas and which, perhaps half-unconsciously, he knew he needed for the creative ferment of his mind.

After a year, Delaunay's military service came to an end: he was excused from his second year of service and discharged.

He returned to Paris, where things had changed in the meantime. The late work of Cézanne, to which the Salon d'Automne had devoted a great retrospective show in 1907, and the discovery of Negro sculpture and ancient Iberian art had led certain artists into new avenues of abstract thought. These influences had altered their relationship to the visible and initiated a re-evaluation of all categories of art. Georges Braque and Picasso had been the first to paint Cubist pictures. Their leading role as carriers of new ideas began to emerge; and whenever painters, collectors, and writers met, the new phenomenon became the main topic of conversation. Spiritual ferment and unrest pervaded the artistic climate and new horizons seemed to open up, creating a tense atmosphere of expectancy and creative productivity.

By 1908, the Bateau Lavoir group had been formed at 13 Rue Ravignan, in Montmartre. It was a new creative center with Picasso, Max Jacob, and Juan Gris among its members. Braque, Apollinaire, the mathematician Maurice Princet, and many others visited it constantly. In 1907, Daniel-Henry Kahnweiler had opened his gallery on the Rue Vignon and begun to show and promote the new pictures. In November, 1908, this gallery gave the first Braque show. It was on this occasion that the critic Louis Vauxcelles used the word *cubes*, and while he meant it in a derogatory sense, his epithet stuck and became the name for a new art style. Wilhelm Uhde's gallery and Gertrude Stein's house served as gathering places for people, ideas, and pictures.

Though Delaunay was a frequent guest at Gertrude Stein's, and though he often visited Uhde in his gallery (in 1907, he had painted a Neoimpressionist portrait of Uhde), he knew Picasso and Braque only superficially. No close contact ever developed between him and these two artists. In Gertrude Stein's memoirs, Delaunay gets only a brief mention: "Delaunay himself was amusing. He was fairly able and inordinately ambitious. He was always asking how old Picasso had been when he had painted a certain picture. When he was told he always said, oh I am not as old as that yet. I will do as much when I am that age. . . . He used to come a great deal to the Rue de Fleurus. Gertrude Stein used to delight in him."[7]

One day, Gertrude Stein mischievously referred to Rousseau as the "poor man's Cézanne." Delaunay never forgave her that remark.

There are self-portraits by Delaunay from the years 1906–7, 1908, and 1909. They not only give us an idea of what he looked like at the time but also show how his attitude toward himself changed from year to year and how his artistic approach changed during that important period. In the *Self-Portrait with Japanese Print* of about 1905 (fig. 37), in which Delaunay made himself look "half-worker, half-Bohemian," the stylized self, the intensification of form, and the pale, dull coloring all belong together. The self-portrait study of 1906 (fig. 38) is very different, with its brightness and strong coloring. The winning, self-assured good looks, youthfulness, and elegance of the charming young man seem to have come to life in the fresh, loose, and highly effective technique in which we can detect a touch of Fauvism. The self-portrait of 1908 (fig. 39) is by comparison muted in expression and color; the attitude toward the self is more matter-of-fact; the whole is characterized by greater simplicity and naturalness. In the diamond pattern of the background we recognize –

is signed or dated, one may well assume that Delaunay himself considered them mere preliminary studies.

The pictures show flowers, tree blossoms, foliage, and stems, mostly seen from very close and against dark backgrounds. While they exhibit Delaunay's strong and genuine gift for observation, they are also full of a mysterious poetry. The sense of something precious and intimate which they convey reminds us of the two still lifes entitled *Vases and Objects* done a year earlier. As glimpses into the realm of nature, they are suffused with a feeling for all organic, soundlessly moving life. Delaunay's ability to get close to living things, to understand them from inside, as it were, through tender and living sympathy, is manifest in these pictures.

This deep empathy with the organic life of nature produces in some of these flower paintings (like *Begonias No. 59*) kinds of forms of which it is hard to say whether they are entirely the result of observation or represent pictorial thought structures – groups of circular forms which, in their axial arrangement, seem to anticipate his *Moon* pictures and even his *Rhythm without End* series. No doubt his profound observation of nature in miniature led him, perhaps without his own conscious knowledge, to certain basic forms and structures which were later to take on a life of their own in his work.

Chaville lies on the southwestern periphery of Paris. From there, a short walk in the direction of the city takes you to the park of Saint-Cloud. There are two pictures Delaunay painted in that park (figs. 7, 48). In the deep, muted color nuances of their quick, broad brush strokes, which often let the empty canvas show through near the edges, Cézanne's influence is again apparent. These pictures are more formal, more abstract than the flower studies, but they have the same intimate character. The Saint-Cloud pictures also offer insights into vegetative life. The structure of the small flower pictures seems to have been transferred to these larger ones, where it has a more architectural effect. The individual sections of foliage are greatly simplified and combined in a way that gives them the somewhat alien look of exotic foreign leaf shapes; their umbrella-like curve overarches in rhythmic motion the shady hollows whose negative form is fully realized. The palette of dark and somewhat lighter green, of brown-gray in contrast with the whitish blue-violet of the sky forms a harmony of exquisite taste, expressing to perfection the elegance of that quiet old park.

When Robert and Sonia knew that they belonged together, and wanted to marry and pursue their goals together, Sonia asked Uhde for a divorce. "After a year, our marriage came to end," wrote Uhde. "A friend of mine felt that he could make my wife more perfectly happy than I could; it did not occur to me to stand in the way of a beautiful future for her."[8]

Sonia and Robert Delaunay were married in November, 1910. Inspired by his growing love and by the new experience, Delaunay painted (in 1909) a picture which, with its color and atmosphere, form and format, still belongs to his previous work, but whose theme shows for the first time, and in a visionary flash, the motif of the Eiffel Tower (fig. 52). This picture marks the end of his youthful efforts. At the same time, it contains and heralds his mature work that was yet to come.

The Tower stands framed by irregular, jagged dark clouds, a slender, beautifully symmetrical shape fading somberly into the sky. Its elegant slate-color silhouette floats almost exactly in the center of the picture in deep, densely atmospheric space, against a background of bluish-gray and greenish-ocher clouds whose spasmodic surface rhythm is like uncanny heat lightning.

Despite its small format, the picture has a meaningful and mysterious air of visionary greatness.

Delaunay painted it for his wife-to-be. "It was 'our' picture," she says of it. "The Eiffel Tower and the universe were one and the same to him." The upper corners contain these words in his handwriting:

Exposition	Mouvement
Universelle 1889	Profondeur 1909
La Tour à l'Univers s'adresse	France-Russie

("Universal Exposition 1889 / The Tower calls out to the Universe / Movement / Depth 1909 / France–Russia")

Whenever Delaunay discussed his work in later years, he referred to the series of Saint-Séverin pictures as the first truly valid examples of his work, the starting point for his subsequent development (see plate 2; figs. 8–11; p. 70). As a matter of fact, the interior of the church which he painted in 1909 soon became famous, especially in Germany. The first version of this subject was shown at the first exhibition of the Blaue Reiter in Munich in 1911–12, and it appears in the Blaue Reiter yearbook of 1912. It was bought by the painter Adolf Erbslöh. Not only did the picture have a demonstrable influence on Paul Klee and Marianne von Werefkin; it also had a general, almost shocklike effect on all of German Expressionism. This effect even made itself felt in the "Gothic" aspects of the film *The Cabinet of Doctor Caligari*.

There are seven versions of the picture. Four were painted in 1909 and two in 1909–10. Another version, begun in 1908–9, was taken up again in 1915, worked over in a different technique and in accordance with Delaunay's later color ideas, and completed with new elements. These are his first paintings in a larger format and the first series of differing versions of the same subject. This peculiarity of his working method is basic to Delaunay's entire later production. He was sure that it is far more important to repeat the same motif over and over until ultimate clarity is achieved than to paint twenty different pictures. Of course, there are many different creative processes at work within any such series: the artist may be varying the motif continually until he has "exhausted" it, or else he may get closer and closer to his goal by taking a different starting point each time. There are series which Delaunay completed in uninterrupted sequence, and others to which he returned at different times of his life, always with a new approach.

The ancient Gothic Church of Saint-Séverin stands in the Rue des Prêtres Saint-Séverin. Delaunay's pictures show the view through a row of columns from the right aisle toward the cloister window. It is important to know that Delaunay did not paint these pictures in the church but in his studio. However, he did make several sketches in Saint-Séverin.

While Delaunay's earlier pictures showed either his interpretation of an established style or the influence of certain predecessors, the Saint-Séverin group constitute his first original pictorial creation. They are not derived from any other work in the history of art. What is new here – apart from the larger format – is the interplay of three-dimensional volume and linear elements. The dynamics of the pictures are determined by the distortion of the vertical, which makes the massive columns look as if they were seen in a concave mirror – just the way the retina receives impressions before they are corrected by our consciousness. The inner space of the side aisle becomes a bent ellipsoid.

This curvature of space inside Saint-Séverin anticipates something that was to become of paramount importance to Delaunay: his doctrine of the roundness of all things. He saw those columns as curves. "I have never in my life seen a straight line," he said in later years. "They look as if they were straight, but they never are straight. When I was young, I got into trouble often enough because I painted all my houses at an angle, the way I saw them."[9]

This optical law, dredged up into consciousness and turned into a creative principle, is fundamental to the Saint-Séverin pictures. In Germany, the resulting distortion was later interpreted as a pathetico-mystical intention.

The nearly monochromatic color scheme – blue and green in strong contrasts of light and dark within the blue scale – models the three-dimensional structures. This reduction of color in favor of tridimensionality places the pictures (with reservations) near early Cubism. The monochromatic scheme is interrupted in only two places by warmer accents. The light, streaming in from the right, produces bright reddish and orange facets on the floor which are reflected in the vaults. Here we see for the first time how light is materialized in prismatic color forms. In this way the flat surface is broken, so to speak, into three-dimensional chunks.

In connection with a book he planned to write about himself, Delaunay put down a series of comments on his most important pictures. Some of these notes are dated 1924, others 1938–39. His remarks on the Saint-Séverin series are on the back of a photograph of his third version, which is today in the Solomon R. Guggenheim Museum in New York City:

In *Saint-Séverin* there is a will toward construction, but the form is traditional. The *brisures* (refractions of light) seem timid. The light fractures the lines in the arches and on the floor. The color is still light-dark, though I had not wanted to copy nature objectively, and this still results in perspective. As with Cézanne, the contrasts are *binary* (in two parts) and

Eiffel Tower 1910

not *simultaneous*. The reaction of color is carried by the line. The modulation is still the *classical form* in the sense of the expressive métier.

The picture shows a definite desire for a new form but does not achieve it.

Great influence on Expressionism, on the film *Caligari*, on the Russian theater.

The total movement of the picture finds its continuation in my later work.[10]

The artist who wrote these lines was the creator of the late *Rhythm without End*, looking back over his development and considering this early picture his starting point.

The Saint-Séverin series shows only minor variations. The last version, the seventh, begun in Paris and reworked in wax in Madrid in 1915, combines the original formal conception with a new sense of color (plate 2). The palette consists of the colors of the spectrum, which transform the gloomy vault into a space filled with light; in place of the prismatic light facets on the floor, there are circular light forms that anticipate the inventions of the year 1912.

During the summer of 1909, Delaunay had begun work on two subjects: *The Dirigible and the Tower* (fig. 49) and *The Spire of Notre-Dame* (figs. 50, 51). In his estate, there is a picture post card showing the dirigible *République* either taking off or landing (see p. 108). Undoubtedly he bought the card in a moment of enthusiasm for the event. In depicting the characteristic silhouette, he obviously leaned on this photograph. The small picture (fig. 49) – only 13³/₄ inches by 10¹/₂ inches – shows the dirigible at the same angle (diagonally from behind) against the dark outline of the Eiffel Tower. A tree, on the right, cuts across it and seems to capture it in its branches. It is remarkable what a still-life effect the artist has produced by combining these massive objects. The few colors harmonize smoothly and form a dusky atmosphere in which the airship floats like a mysterious silent monster in front of the Eiffel Tower, the *Tour-Univers*. And while all emotion has been eliminated, the technical world has been elevated into poetry.

Delaunay painted the spire of Notre-Dame several times more in later years, looking from the top of the left tower of the cathedral toward the bend in the Seine. The composition of the first version is obviously based on a post card of this famous sight (see p. 108). Delaunay was a confirmed collector of post cards and photographs, and they often served him as inspiration. He owned whole stacks of them, especially photos of unusual technical sights, streets of Paris, airplanes, sporting scenes, bird's-eye views of Paris, panoramas, and views of the Eiffel Tower. Sonia Delaunay reports

that even in later years, he always carried packs of his favorite post cards in his pockets.

He was full of boyish enthusiasm for photography and its new technical possibilities. For his composition of the *The Spire of Notre-Dame*, the view shown on the photograph was all he needed – we do not know, and it is not essential to the question of his work, whether he also made sketches of his own from the same spot. But when we compare his picture with the actual view, we see how Delaunay subjected everything in that panorama to an angular, rhythmical surface pattern.

In his first small Eiffel Tower, *The Tower* of 1909 (fig. 52) with the inscription "La Tour à l'Univers s'adresse," the grandiose theme of his life made its first appearance: "The Eiffel Tower – barometer of my art."[11] It meant much more to him than just another picture subject; all his life, the Eiffel Tower remained a magic-laden symbol for communication with the entire world. Art was the content of Delaunay's life, but not only in a private way. To him, painting had universal significance:

Painting had a general human value for Delaunay. While its means are pictorial, it transcends the pictorial in its meaning. It is essential for the life of nations. Modern man is the man of electricity, of aviation, of speed and motion: the depth of his art is the symbol for the sum total of human activities. This new power of man which penetrates the mysteries of life, of light, makes all works of art universal. A brush stroke made in Paris today is equally valid in the Antipodes – and indeed, the first echoes provoked by Delaunay's work came from Saint Petersburg, Berlin, and New York. For Delaunay, the new art had to usher in the brotherhood of nations.[12]

In the years 1909 to 1911, the Eiffel Tower dominated Delaunay's thoughts. He was continuously busy with it. Before he began his monumental representations, he studied it from above and below, inside and out, from near and far, by day and by night. He absorbed its every mood, perspective, and light effect. In a chapter on "The Eiffel Tower" which is dedicated to Delaunay, the poet Blaise Cendrars wrote:

As soon as I could leave, I went to the Tower with Delaunay. Here is our trip around and in the Eiffel Tower:

None of the known techniques of art can claim to have solved the pictorial problem of the Eiffel Tower. Realism diminishes it; the ancient laws of Italian perspective attenuate it. The Tower rises above Paris, slim as a hat pin. When we moved away from it, it dominated Paris, stiff and perpendicular; when we approached it, it tilted and leaned over us. Seen from the first platform, it spiraled upward; seen from the top, it sank into itself with straddling legs and indrawn neck. Delaunay wanted to show Paris simultaneously, to incorporate the Tower into its surroundings. We tried every vantage point, we studied it from different angles, from all sides. Its sharpest profile can be seen from the top of the Passerelle de Passy.

And those thousands of tons of iron, those almost seven hundred feet of girders and beams, those four arches spanning three hundred feet, that whole dizzying mass flirted with us. On some spring days, it was lithe and gay, and coquettishly opened its cloud screen for us. On other days, in bad weather, it was ill-tempered, sulky, and obstinate; it seemed to be freezing. At midnight, we no longer existed for it: its lights were all aimed at New York. Even then it flirted with New York; and at noon it set the time for ships on the high seas.... And as we wandered around it, we discovered that it exerted a strange attraction on many people.... So many viewpoints for coming to terms with the Eiffel Tower. But Delaunay wanted to interpret it pictorially. He succeeded, at last, with the magnificent picture we all know. He cut it open at the joints in order to fit it into the frame; he foreshortened and tilted it to let it have its full dizzy seven hundred feet; he grasped it from different angles, in fifteen different perspectives – one part is seen from below, another from above; the houses surrounding it have been taken from the right, from the left, in bird's-eye view, and seen from the ground up....[13]

Cendrars met Delaunay in November, 1912, at a time when the great Eiffel Tower pictures that were to become so famous had already been finished. Cendrars was inspired by them and wrote a poem in homage to them in August, 1913.

The earliest of the big pictures is the *Eiffel Tower with Trees* (fig. 12), painted in 1909. The format is larger than that of most of the Sainte-Séverins; the picture is 49⁷/₈″ high. This is the only version that shows the Tower in nature: there is a tree in the foreground, reminiscent of the Saint-Cloud pictures, and the sky is filled with clusters of small clouds. In contrast to the tree, which stands at a natural angle, the Tower is seen on a slant; this makes it seem strangely in motion, reaching upward. While we get a frontal view throughout, there is a rhythmical alternation between birds-eye and worm's-eye view; we seem to be looking now up, now down at the various sections – a vertical aggregate of viewpoints which of course distorts the appearance of the Tower. It seems to be built up in a rush of successive viewpoints, and from this succession there clearly emerges an element of time, heretofore an unknown dimension in pictorial representation. The whole thing is happening in a space that still has an atmospheric quality. Everything seems bathed in a mother-of-pearl light which reduces the colors of objects to brownish and bluish grays. To the right of the Tower there are brick-red color zones which are *of* it though they are separate from it. The special magic of this first great effort consists, among other things, in the precise and sensitive harmony of three different movements: the tree reaching upward in soft, large rhythms; the angular push and crowding of the Tower shapes; and finally, the syncopated explosion of balloon-shaped cloudlets.

From April to September, 1910, Delaunay and his wife-to-be lived in the quiet solitude of La Cluse, near Nantua. Their rooms gave on a balcony which Robert used as a studio. Here and later in Paris, he painted the famous, dynamic, light-shattering Eiffel Tower pictures of 1910.

These pictures have been dispersed throughout the world. In that sense, Delaunay's goal of establishing contact with the universe has been achieved. Only if all these pictures were placed side by side – which is no longer possible – would it become obvious how much strength and passion Delaunay invested in his dramatic struggle with this subject, what roads he traveled in order to conquer "those thousands of tons of iron" spiritually and pictorially. Perhaps the most tragic stage in this process is that which shows the number of differing horizontal and vertical viewpoints so greatly multiplied that the Tower, cut apart and shattered, collapses into itself (fig. 53). Added to the numerous external views is a further dimension – the physical sense of being inside, above, and beneath the thousand-fold girders and connecting braces. This attempt takes Delaunay to the boundaries of the possible. "I tried to place a variety of viewpoints in spatial relation to each other. It was a search for total form, in which I failed because I was caught in the transition from traditional painting to the new reality."[14]

At that time, he also made a new discovery. He had studied the work of Cézanne with utmost admiration; Cézanne meant more to him than any other painter. "Cézanne above all had a presentiment of new horizons, but his troubled and restless artist's life did not allow him to find the means of steering for them. But in Cézanne's last watercolors – what transparency striving toward a supernatural beauty, beyond anything we had seen before!"[15]

Cézanne's later watercolors led Delaunay to the observation that the incidence of rays of light in nature actually obliterates the outlines of objects, breaking the continuity of the line and thus destroying the object. In following this observation to its logical conclusion, Delaunay felt he was acting as Cézanne's successor. It was at this juncture that the destruction of the object became a necessity for him. Hand in hand with this destruction, however, went the gradual establishment of the autonomous order and movement of light.

In Germany, the most famous Eiffel Tower picture – which Delaunay himself considered the most important of the series – belonged to the Köhler collection in Berlin. The well-known collector Bernhard Köhler bought it at the opening of the first Blaue Reiter show in Munich toward the end of 1911. It was displayed on a full page of the Blaue Reiter yearbook, and quickly became – along with *Saint-Séverin* – representative of Delaunay's work in German eyes. The painting was destroyed in a wartime fire in 1945.

The Eiffel Tower appeared there in a framework of architecture, between and high above a welter of building sections and roofs. The same view would be utilized in later versions. This powerful work marks the first time Delaunay presented the form-shattering incidence of light. Although again the Tower was seen from many vantage points at once, and its lower portion was sliced open toward the picture plane, the actual event that gave form to this picture was the action of light. Light cut away entire sections of the whole, or obliterated them by means of blinding radiance.

In the later large versions of this theme, done in 1910–11, the effect of light becomes more and more the determining factor for the picture (see plate 4). The number of vantage points is reduced, and the Tower appears more rigidly upright; at the same time, there is a broadening of the paths of light, those ribbons of brightness that dominate the picture surface. They attack the object and obliterate its contours by cutting across them. Tension ensues between object and light. Where this tension is most masterfully controlled, the picture achieves a balance between the two elements by means of dynamic interpenetration – as, for instance, in the version now at the Kunstmuseum in Basel (plate 3). "The Tower is not the result of calculation; it is a being that rises out of itself. The light helps it rise by means of opposing 'zones' in which it is fractured and which carry the Tower along with it in a riot of energy and constant action."[16]

A series of six large pen-and-ink drawings dated 1910 (see pp. 2, 12, 27) shows how Delaunay attacked the problem of dovetailing the object disintegrating in light – the Eiffel Tower, a giant ferris wheel – with the emerging new light order. In their spontaneous, excited line vibrates something of the elemental power of the action which fragmentizes the visible and lends concrete shape to the invisible. The drawings differ from each other only in thoroughness of execution and degree of object destruction. More important than these differences is the fact that in all of them certain rhythms recur in more and more fundamental form, indicating that Delaunay had begun to work his way closer and closer to a predesigned artistic scheme.

The paths of light which cut diagonally across the picture, severing the physical unity of the Tower on their way, setting its fragments against each other, and creating blinding zones between eye and object, are unquestionably based on intent observation. But there are too those swinging arcs on the left, touching one another along a diagonal axis. This is the same constellation which we have noted in one of his begonia sketches done at Chaville, and from which the motif of his moons would emerge in 1913. This form to which Delaunay clung so tenaciously did not originate in observation; nor is it the result of a merely formal rhythm. What emerges here is a basic structure characteristic of his work. The structural values which Delaunay developed out of a rhythm that has become autonomous and independent of any object, and out of the large diamond shapes that result from the intersection of light paths, go far beyond the large Eiffel Tower paintings. They point the way towards the *fenêtres*, the window pictures. The pen-and-ink Eiffel Towers must be considered Delaunay's most important known drawings.

Delaunay's most radical approach to the contest between light and object is an Eiffel Tower painting currently at Essen (plate 4). Blindingly bright light streams down from above like a cataract, eliminating the Tower's physical reality and position in space. The Tower becomes a dark, swaying apparition seen against the light.

In the first several versions, the big problem was to conquer the structure by means of perspective through all possible dimensions and aspects. This problem receded in the measure that the activity of light became more and more important as the actual picture subject. In this process, the physical reality of the Eiffel Tower disintegrates, and at the end, completely dissolved by the superior force of light, it remains a mere passive shadow.

Thus Delaunay carried his first great pictorial idea to the very limit of what was artistically possible at that

screens. The over-all color effect remains diffuse; we get the impression of delicate-hued, floating transparency. The pure, rich color makes its appearance in small, timid details. It is a part of the construction but has not yet developed its own organizing power.

In this painting, we find all the elements assembled that are to be synthesized in Delaunay's window pictures of the following years. The influences of Cézanne and Seurat meet in a composition that has been carried to the very boundary of the representational – a composition created according to its own laws, out of the inspired idea of the pictorializing reality of light.

Since 1909, Delaunay had been living and working in a state of incredible high creative tension. He was painting like a man possessed. This was one of the most intensely productive periods of his life. Each of the three years was rich and full, but each had its own creative keynote. If the year 1909 saw him under the direct experience of the variety and richness of light, conceiving the basic themes of his later work, 1910 – the year of the Eiffel Towers – was a time of passionately explosive *Sturm und Drang:* the struggle with an overpowering theme against which he tested and increased his own power to the utmost. The year 1911 brought a transformation. The subjective-spontaneous approach was abandoned; he sought for laws. Confined to a single theme, he tried to explore and logically develop the means that could express his experience of the world.

Individual in their expression though they are, the pictures of those years can easily be fitted into the framework of their time. They lie along the line of transition from Cézanne to Cubism. While the views of the park of Saint-Cloud, the first small *Tour-Univers,* and *The Dirigible and the Tower* in their soft and muted color tones are guided by Cézanne's palette, the dark, almost monochromatic coloring of the Saint-Séverin series and the early City pictures show elements of early Cubism along with a growing three-dimensional structuring. The multiplying viewpoints of the Eiffel Towers also indicate a certain preoccupation with Cubist problems. On the other hand, in his more and more intense observation of the action of light and its effect on the object *(brisures),* Delaunay returned to the light refractions of the late Cézanne. Delaunay himself called this period his *époque destructive,* his destructive period:[20] lines are broken, the object is destroyed. The strict Cubists effected this destruction by way of a progressive analysis and dissection of the object, first into three-dimensional values, then into areas and lines. Delaunay, who had begun with this method, shifted the destructive attack more and more toward refracting light to show the dynamic effect of light itself. The destruction of objects and the creation of new pictorial forms through light are one and the same process. With the realization that light materializes in color forms, he turned away from Cubism and struck out on his own road, giving his art a new basis.

Just at the time when Delaunay's research began to go beyond the boundaries of Cubism, his name as a supporter of and fighter for Cubism was brought before the public: the famous 1911 exhibition of the Indépendants at the Quai d'Orsay, in which the Cubists first appeared as a group in the Salle 41, caused a scandal which exposed the names of Metzinger, Henri Le Fauconnier, Léger, Gris, Delaunay, and Gleizes (at that time Picasso and Braque were exhibiting only at Kahnweiler's gallery) to the cross fire of public controversy. Delaunay was represented by the Eiffel Tower picture which later reached the Köhler collection in Berlin, the version of *The City* which today is in the Musée National d'Art Moderne (fig. 15), and a third picture called *Paris Landscape* which can no longer be identified today.

Delaunay's son Charles (see p. 89) was born in January, 1911. The marriage of Robert Delaunay and Sonia Delaunay-Terk was more than a human bond between two artistic personalities. It was for many years the basis of a collaboration of the highest creative productivity in which it is often hard to tell who produced the first spark, though Robert was most often the leading force, especially in the decisive early years. While he was the poet, the "constructor," the inventor who offered the revelations of the métier to his wife, her own strong nature contributed an absolutely elementary feeling for color which also influenced his color style. Sonia's sense of steadfastness and discipline was instrumental in getting Delaunay to finish his pictures, which he had often left unfinished before. Thus "the Delaunays" later became a well-established name in Paris which stood not only for his inventions and pictorial ideas but also for her new creations in the field of painting, design, and fashion. For at the core of all their artistic statements lay a great basic idea: to find a new way – beyond the boundaries of painting – to express the totality of modern life through color.

From the beginning of his union with Sonia, Delaunay knew that he no longer stood alone with his ideas, ambitions, and concepts. She understood him, she believed in him, she gave him the deep sense of himself which he needed for his development. During the first years of their marriage, she occupied herself chiefly with color applications and embroideries, which incidentally also served to lend a personal and colorful note to their dwelling. It was at this early date that Sonia began to put her feeling for color in interior design – which was to become famous – into practice. Step by step, she modernized their apartment, which had originally been furnished in Empire style: she added new color, and covered the figured wallpaper with white cotton cloth, which made the paintings stand out beautifully; she replaced the old-fashioned lamp shades with new ones she had made herself; cushions with colorful appliqués that pointed to her later collages gave the rooms special accents.

In contrast to most artists, the Delaunays had a well-maintained, well-regulated household. Sonia's income from her Russian fortune permitted them to live in elegant style, with servants and a fine cuisine. Every Sunday was their at-home day. The apartment on the Rue des Grands Augustins gradually attracted painters and poets. A circle of friends formed around Delaunay. One of its members was the painter Elisabeth Epstein, who had been a friend of Sonia's for years. She had lived in Munich, had studied there, and knew Kandinsky well; and she had kept in touch with him after she got to Paris.

It was Elisabeth Epstein who, after the 1911 exhibition of the Indépendants, enthusiastically reported to Kandinsky about Delaunay's work. In October, 1911, she sent him photographs of the paintings. They reached Kandinsky in Murnau as he was feverishly working on the preparations for the book *Der Blaue Reiter* with Franz Marc and August Macke. His reaction to the photos was spontaneous. On October 28, 1911, Kandinsky wrote to Delaunay:

Sir,

I thank you for sending me the photos (via Madame Epstein). Your pictures interest me *greatly*. I have had a halftone made of your *Eiffel Tower* (is this title correct?), and it has come out very well. I will send you *Der Blaue Reiter*, which is to be published in January. Would you perhaps write down a few thoughts about your aims in art? Perhaps about Cubism? Whichever you prefer![21]

In the first days of December, 1911, Kandinsky and Marc, after a passionately controversial jury meeting in which battle lines were clearly drawn, together walked out on the Neue Künstlervereinigung München – the New Artist's Association of Munich – and instantly began preparations for the first showing of the Blaue Reiter group, which was to open in the Galerie Thannhauser in Munich on December 18, 1911. Kandinsky hastened to request pictures by Delaunay for this show; they arrived on the day the show opened. "Fortunately, all is well; the show is being hung today, and your four paintings have just arrived." (December 18, 1911.)

The pictures were *Saint-Séverin No. 1*, 1909; *The City No. 2*, 1909–10; *Eiffel Tower*, 1910; *The City*, 1911; and one drawing.

In the same letter, Kandinsky also thanked Delaunay for sending him a picture by Rousseau which he wanted to buy.

Two days later, he joyfully announced: "In haste! Your *Saint-Séverin* is sold. A good beginning! I am very glad, and I congratulate you." The buyer was the painter Adolf Erbslöh. And on the same day, a few hours later, came the news that Alexej von Jawlensky had bought *The City* and that, besides, Bernhard Köhler was interested in the *Eiffel Tower*. The postscript of the letter says: "The artists who took part in the 'Blaue Reiter'

intellectual curiosity drove him everywhere something new was happening. He was open to all new trends, no matter where they originated; he accepted and assimilated them, enriched them with his own ideas, and wrote brilliant essays and reviews about exhibits, painters, and trends in his polished, poetic French. "He is the advocate of everything modern, everything new, of every avant-garde movement that wants to abolish outmoded concepts; in encouraging and promoting these new trends, Apollinaire develops the most intensive activity."[24]

Apollinaire was a personality with a thousand facets: charming wag, *bon vivant* and gourmet, dreamy and melancholy poet "who thought himself ill-liked," unreliable and helpful, brilliant in his eloquence, he always formed a center around which friends and listeners gathered, without whom he could not live.

For Apollinaire, who had been friends with Picasso, Braque, Max Jacob, André Salmon, and others since the Bateau Lavoir days, Cubism was the epitome of the new, the vital, the promising in art. Owing to their verbal brilliance, his critiques in *Le Temps* and *L'Intransigeant* and his many magazine articles were a powerful voice in the service of modern developments.

Delaunay and Apollinaire became acquainted in 1911. Delaunay sometimes visited him in his apartment on the Rue Gros and later on the Rue Lafontaine. At Apollinaire's he also met the novelist Élémir Bourges, an older man and a member of the Académie, and Fernand Fleuret, Apollinaire's constant companion. In September, 1911, Apollinaire had the misfortune of being suspected as an accomplice in the theft of the *Mona Lisa* from the Louvre; he even spent a week in jail. It took months for him to clear his name; during that time many of his friends kept away from him and his enemies used this opportunity to attack him sharply. Robert and Sonia Delaunay were among the few who stood by him during those months, and he became a frequent guest at the apartment on the Rue des Grands Augustins. During one of the visits, Delaunay did the half-finished portrait study in brown and gray which, though only the hair, forehead, and half of the face are painted, brilliantly characterizes Apollinaire.

In January, 1912, Delaunay spent a month in Laon with his wife and their one-year-old son. They were joined by the landscape painter Lotiron, with whom Delaunay had served in the army in 1908. During those weeks in the familiar but newly experienced environment, Delaunay painted a number of oil studies of Laon, street scenes and especially views of the

cathedral, whose shape had fascinated him in earlier years.

The group of Laon pictures comprises three larger ones, showing street views, and several views of the cathedral. Except for the large version of *The Towers of Laon* (plate 6), which he may have finished after his return to Paris, these are lightly and loosely painted studies from nature, free from the formal problems of his last *City* pictures. They adhere closely to the actual motif, and through their atmospheric values give a perfect impression of the little town's wintry mood and the transparency of the air. Very evocative is the *Street in Laon*, seen at dusk (fig. 18). With its solitary street lamp, its whitish-blue sky, and its division into rectangular zones, it recalls the work of Roger de la Fresnaye. The rhythmic motion of the view toward the cathedral (fig. 19) rises and falls with the zigzag design of the street. The brush stroke is lively, swift, and precise; the colors are muted. "I am fairly well satisfied with my last studies on this motif," he wrote to Sam Halpert after his return. "It is now time for you to make fun of my love of the country, of easels, etc.; in the depth of winter in the beautiful town of Laon: what bold colors in nature at that season and in that place!"[25]

The acme of the Laon paintings is the large view of *The Towers of Laon* at the Musée National d'Art Moderne (plate 6). It was preceded by a lively and angularly rhythmical study which is now owned by the Kunsthalle in Hamburg (fig. 20). The study shows a somewhat narrower view; this makes its agglomeration of roof tops more concentrated and dynamic, more immediate than it appears in the larger picture. The latter tones down these three-dimensional values but raises the entire scene toward a serene monumentality, intensifies it by adding foreground and a curving street, and individualizes the tower by means of architectural details. This feeling of distance helps Delaunay achieve magnificent spatial movement. The upside-down facets in the sky correspond with the cubic forms of the architecture, especially of the square tower. This results in a crystalline rhythm of color zones which pervades the entire picture – sky, roof tops, and foreground – and lends a disembodied, transparent basic note to the whole.

One night during his stay in Laon, Delaunay struck up an acquaintance with a high-school teacher he met in a restaurant. The professor turned out to be the famous writer Jules Romain. Their acquaintance continued in Paris.

Early in February, 1912, Delaunay and his family returned to Paris, where a great deal of work awaited him. At the end of the month, he was to have his first one-man show at the Galerie Barbazanges; Marie Laurencin, Apollinaire's friend, had been invited to contribute a few of her pictures to the show. The catalog of the exhibition lists forty-one pictures by Delaunay from the years 1904 to 1912. It was, in short, a regular retrospective. The preface to the catalog was written by the mathematician Maurice Princet, a friend of Delaunay's since 1911 and one of his most intelligent and fruitful partners in conversations about painting problems. In it Princet, who was trained in precision and abstraction and had an intense feeling for art, clearly outlines Delaunay's development and the intellectual power behind his pictorial ideas:

> His vibrant temperament and a truly French vital energy are coupled with the most rigorous discipline in researching his methods. Métier . . . seems to him the essential work of the artist. . . .
>
> When Delaunay discusses, argues, compares, and deduces, he always does so with palette in hand. His reasoning is not merely a dazzling acrobatic display of brilliant paradoxes; his ideas . . . lead him simply and naturally to pictorial reality, to colors and lines. He expresses himself in volumes and color values; he defends his earlier works with new ones which explain the preceding ones. . . . His sensitivity has not been diminished by his technical researches; on the contrary, it has been purified, refined, and strengthened without losing any of its freshness.[26]

It is typical of the period that art and science tried to interpenetrate each other in the spirit of modernity:

> In those years, whole treasures of patience, analysis, research, and scholarship were used up in the studios of the young painters in Paris, and never before had there been such a conflagration of intelligence! The painters studied everything: contemporary art, all periods of style, the artistic output of all peoples, theories of all times. Never before had so many painters been observed going to museums to see and study the techniques of the old masters and compare them with each other. One studied the pictorial creations of savages belonging to primitive tribes and the pictorial traces of prehistoric man. At the same time, there was intense interest in the scientific theories of electrochemistry, biology, experimental psychology, and applied physics. Two men who were not themselves painters had an enormous influence on the Cubists: the mathematician Princet, who imposed mathematical formulas on every new picture he was shown; and the learned Hellenist Chaudois, who tested all established theories against quotes from Aristotle and the pre-Socratics.

This mad critical and creative activity was called by Maurice Raynal "the search for the fourth dimension."[27]

On March 20, 1912, the Indépendants were to have their opening. The show at the Galerie Barbazanges in February had been so important for Delaunay as his first chance to demonstrate his entire development that he had gathered up every obtainable picture for it (including even the *Eiffel Tower* he had sold in Germany). For the Indépendants, he had to create something new. There was not enough time for several pictures. He therefore decided to bring together the themes of his most recent years in a single large composition. In the amazingly short time of only fifteen days,[28] Delaunay painted the huge picture *The City of Paris* (plate 5) for this exhibition. The work measures almost nine feet in height and more than thirteen feet in width. It is now in the Musée National d'Art Moderne. It represents a kind of synthesis and at the same time an apotheosis of the time in his life which he himself called his "destructive period."

> Apollinaire wrote in *L'Intransigeant* of March 19, 1912: Delaunay's painting is by far the most important one of this Salon. *The City of Paris* is more than an artistic manifestation. This picture marks the rebirth of an artistic concept which may have been lost since the days of the great Italian masters. And while it summarizes the total intention of the artist who painted it, it also summarizes, without scientific pretension, the total intention of modern art. It is executed on a grand scale. The composition is simple and noble. And any argument against it cannot deny this truth: this is a picture, truly a picture, and it has been a long time since we have seen one of those.

What gives this work its feeling of festive representation in the grand style – and therefore its eminently French character – is the inclusion of the famous ancient theme of the three Graces in the view of a modern metropolis. The unself-consciousness with which Delaunay has taken this Classic motif and incorporated it into the modern spirit is similar to that of earlier generations who sprinkled the same city with Classicist statues, thus continuing the heritage of antiquity. The combination of these two spheres lends an extratemporal quality to the picture.

The proportions have been stretched beyond those of the original design – Delaunay had a photo of a Pompeian fresco of the Graces from which he had made a study as early as 1909 (fig. 54); in this study, on dark ground, only the lighted parts of the bodies are indicated by slanting brush strokes. Although the heads in the painting have the same Cubist character as those in a 1912 study (fig. 55), the motif nevertheless retains

A gouache dated June, 1912 (fig. 56), showing three similarly constructed window motifs side by side, demonstrates what Delaunay had in mind as the final concept of his window pictures: an interlacing of several window views in a differentiated, simultaneously seen whole. This general conception probably explains the complicated subtitles which Delaunay originally gave to the various versions. In the catalog of the first exhibit at which these pictures were shown, they are identified according to the categories *représentation*, *partie*, and *motif* – for example, "Fenêtres ouvertes simultanément. 1ᵉ partie, 3ᵉ motif" – "Simultaneously open windows. 1ˢᵗ part, 3ʳᵈ motif." Later Delaunay eliminated these working subtitles, which only he himself understood.

There are four pictures known today which give us an idea of the total concept of these so-called simultaneous windows. One of them, at the Philadelphia Museum of Art (fig. 22), has the same tripartite scheme as the 1912 gouache and is probably based on it. A third picture, also in three parts and in the form of a horizontal oval, belongs to the Peggy Guggenheim Collection in Venice (fig. 59). It stands out especially because the objective elements in it are almost entirely dissolved in the rhythm of abstract light forms; and the oval shape lends greater unity and concentration to the color rhythms. In Delaunay's own words, "Color phases populate the picture surface in movements of color phenomena that follow and overtake each other. Color is here almost exclusively in its own function, by its contrasts."[40] The curved propeller shape at right makes us assume that this picture was done toward the end of 1912, since the identical shape appears – more centered and with more importance – as a leading motif in the large picture *The Three Windows, the Tower, and the Ferris Wheel*, which we know was completed in December, 1912 (fig. 21).

A final version (fig. 57), in which five window views are placed side by side, completes the series. With this reminiscent lineup of all previous window motifs, Delaunay wrote *finis* to this period in a similarly all-encompassing way as he had done in the spring when he finished his *époque destructive* with the large *City of Paris* (plate 5).

On February 16, 1939, two years before his death, Delaunay gave a talk with slides about his early work to a group of friends. The stenographic record of that occasion conveys the exact words of the fifty-four-year-old Delaunay, the artist of the late, severe pictures, talking about his window pictures more than twenty-five years after he painted them:

But the young Delaunay faced the future full of optimism. That was in 1912. He placed the colors one beside the other – these colors gave him a sense of motion, of joy. He could not yet use them quite correctly; he was still hampered by the exterior subject. Despite everything we believe today, it was what one now calls "abstract" painting – which, by the way, is a very bad word, although it does at least signify a certain purity in painting. We can still distinguish here an indication of a house, here a tower, sky, but it has all been reduced to a pattern. At that time, I believed that one merely had to place pure color on the canvas. But you can see that atavism is very hard to move, even when one has not gone through the École des Beaux-Arts.

In this picture, there are color relations that were not yet known at the time. To define them, I used the term *simultaneous colors*.

I want to explain to you what to my thinking the meaning of these simultaneous contrasts was. Here you have a purple, and here you see a color relation that contrasts with it. This then gives you the beginning of a creation in which there is no hint of a subject, of a landscape. You see here the beginning of a color architecture that is extremely typical, extremely naïve. When I made these simultaneous contrasts, I did not know where to stop. I did not know it and did not see it – I just forged ahead as best I could. I had a way of creating mutual penetration of planes, color modulations, that produced a certain surface and a certain unity. . . .

And he also said, while projecting a color slide of *The Three Windows, the Tower, and the Ferris Wheel* (fig. 21):

I tried for kinds of colored fugues, and I developed the idea as soon as I planned the picture. It is true that one could look at the picture from all sides, but there is of course one view which you might say was the given one. At any rate, you can see the following: this picture differs from all those you saw before. At that time, my friends the Cubists had not yet introduced color into their pictures. I myself saw the need for it then. I was already carrying the idea of movement within myself but could not yet execute it. I felt that color was a dynamic element with its own laws, heights, widths, relationships, complements, dissonances, variations – a whole lot of complicated things which had not yet found expression.

Here, this part . . . this could easily be by Cézanne. And this piece is done in a color scale, not in pure color. This picture, which should not be in my house but in a museum, is called *The Window, the Tower, and the Ferris Wheel*. At that moment, I knew what I wanted to do. The simultaneous contrasts are expressed more violently. Look, for instance, at this

LES FENÊTRES

Du rouge au vert tout le jaune se meurt
Quand chantent les aras dans les forêts natales
Abatis de pi-his
Il y a un poème à faire sur l'oiseau qui n'a qu'une aile
Nous l'enverrons en message téléphonique
Traumatisme géant
Il fait couler les yeux
Voilà une jolie jeune fille parmi les jeunes Turinaises
Le pauvre jeune homme se mouchait dans sa cravate blanche
Tu soulèveras le rideau
Et maintenant voilà que s'ouvre la fenêtre
Araignées quand les mains tissaient la lumière
Beauté pâleur d'insondables violets
Nous tenterons en vain de prendre du repos
On commencera à minuit
Quand on a le temps on a la liberté
Bigorneaux Lottes multiples soleils et l'oursin du couchant
Une vieille paire de chaussures jaunes devant la fenêtre
Tours
Les tours ce sont les rues
Puits
Puits ce sont les places
Puits
Arbres creux qui enlacent les capresses vagabondes
Les Chabins chantent des airs à mourir
Aux Chabines maronnes
Et l'oie oua-oua trompette au nord
Où les chasseurs de ratons
Raclent les pelleteries
Étincelant diamant
Vancouver
Où le train blanc de neige et de feux nocturnes fuit l'hiver
O Paris
Du rouge au vert tout le jaune se meurt
La fenêtre s'ouvre comme une orange
Le beau fruit de la lumière

GUILLAUME APOLLINAIRE

Guillaume Apollinaire's poem "Les Fenetres" ("The Windows"), with handwritten corrections

blue-black, contrasted with a plane of light color tone, a red that is not clear, a warm tone; and here you have a yellow contrasting with a purple, and here you suddenly have the beginning of circular forms. It is strange to look at pictures one painted some time ago. . . .

If an artist has an intuition, he can realize it, but unfortunately only if he works very hard. Here you suddenly see some still representational reminiscences, landscape, houses that might have been painted by a Paris painter like Utrillo, with the giant ferris wheel some of you may not remember, and which is yet another objective element. . . .

In the center of this space, there are certain depths that are produced by color – we might call them planes; but they are not the kind of plane that reminds us of objects of conventional form.

When I had painted this picture, I was not really satisfied, but I felt that I was getting close; for in this picture there are elements of space, of plane, of motion, and apart from these more descriptive elements, which are like hair in the soup for me, there is the over-all design of the picture – an ensemble which has been planned that way, which represents a new creation.

I centered the modulation in this picture quite well, but I was not able to continue it. But look at this kind of propeller: this is the beginning, the seed of what I developed later.

And look at this kind of circular thing which begins to finish off the picture, this kind of color embryo beginning to turn. The color contrasts . . . are beginning to organize themselves – this wants to become a structural ensemble.

And this happened between 1912 and 1913, right in the midst of Cubism.

. . . Of course, today I have to smile a little, for I have gone beyond this – not very far, but still, beyond it. To construct pictures, one must have methods, one must study color scales, the color refractions have to interlace in a tonal harmony. And they have to develop in time; that is, there must be alternating modulations of colors which work against each other and create movement. . . .

In this picture, there is a certain luminosity which harks back to Impressionism. There are little fillers that bespeak a lack of color knowledge, certain weaknesses, to use a harsh word. But it is evident that this road was nevertheless a good road.[41]

The serene remove and modesty of these words with which the later Delaunay harks back to himself as if

to another stand in extreme contrast to the passionate, self-absorbed, tempestuous intensity with which the young Delaunay proclaimed his theses. Temperamental, aggressive, ruthless, he would not tolerate any questioning of or opposition to his ideas. His ways of experiencing and seeing were illuminating and creative, but his creativity did not take place in the silent depths of his awareness; his volcanic, explosive onrush of thought and activity demanded instant realization. The first formulations of his theories were always the best – in their original form, they were something monumentally inspired.

When such a formulation occurred to him, he himself was struck by it, and it put him in a kind of ecstatic delirium; he became more and more carried away with it, talked, extended, explained, surpassed himself, complicating the idea until it became incomprehensible. Infatuated with his theses, he repeated them tirelessly, as passwords and proclamations. This ruffled his relationship with others, for whenever he encountered lack of understanding or opposition, he became vehement, sometimes rude. At the same time, there was something disarming about his youthful naïveté, his absolute honesty and innocence of spirit, his obsession with painting and color. "Robert was 'insane' about color, and I heard him talk about it in strongly erotic terms. He gave himself to it with a kind of physical intoxication still greater than his love of light. Color was an elementary entity to him, and his aversion to neutral tones stemmed from physical revulsion rather than conscious thought."[42]

His rebellious and aggressive manner – no doubt intrinsic in his character – was especially provoked in those years by hostile attacks from the official press and the general public, which objected to everything modern. "The critics tore us to pieces," says Sonia Delaunay. Albert Gleizes and later Bernhard Dorival described the abuse which the press heaped on the heads of progressive painters. This went so far that the government received written complaints that "a public building has been put at the disposal of a band of villains."[43]

Delaunay's inner separation from the Cubists, whose monochrome colors he called "spidery" and whose object analysis he punningly dubbed "cuberie ratiocinante,"[44] resulted in his being attacked by them in turn. They accused him of reverting to Impressionism. Even his best friends – Princet, Apollinaire, and others – were unable to follow Delaunay's thought processes. Gleizes freely admitted that he did not understand the full importance of Delaunay's pictorial discoveries until many years later. Robert observed, "Our first works created a scandal within the realm of formal

Cubism. . . . My colleagues, even those who meant well, did not understand; at every exhibition there reigned an atmosphere of constant strife. Later, after the War of 1914, Albert Gleizes was the only one of my Cubist friends who did me justice, and this justice was really an act of faith on his part."[45]

Indeed, the young Delaunay – supported by Sonia's vital artistic nature – was struggling in various directions: "And if I were to remain alone with my life as a painter, would it not still be worth doing it all in order to be able to live it?"[46]

In addition to those very few friends who stood beside him, Delaunay also found welcome for his work in foreign countries. In the summer of 1912, a young Russian university professor named Smirnoff, an old friend of Sonia's, came from Saint Petersburg to spend two months at La Madeleine. Delaunay gained an understanding and interested companion in him. He could pour out the wealth of his ideas and intuitions to him. Based on these conversations with Delaunay, Smirnoff later gave a lecture on "The Simultaneous" in a Saint Petersburg artists' cabaret called the Brodyatchaya Sobaka, the Stray Dog. The lecture was a rousing success, as Smirnoff reported on a post card. Sonia's colorful "simultaneous" posters decorated the walls.

In the autumn of 1912, the Delaunays learned that the German painters Franz Marc and August Macke were on their way to Paris to visit them. This personal acquaintance dated back to a brief correspondence with Marc on the occasion of the Blaue Reiter show.

Robert and Sonia Delaunay left La Madeleine for Paris to meet them. Delaunay took his newest pictures along, the window series he had painted in La Madeleine. On the same train to Paris was Delaunay's uncle, Charles Damour, who had bought an estate in the nearby Chevreuse Valley where he now lived with his wife. Delaunay had been fond of this family since his childhood. The Damours had been like parents to him. But during recent years, there had been many angry discussions between him and his uncle: Charles Damour, an orthodox follower of the old, conventional school of painting, could neither understand nor tolerate Robert's passionate partisanship of Rousseau and his allegiance to Cézanne and Seurat. Since Robert's temperament made him contradict his uncle vehemently, their relations were often strained. Now, in the train compartment, the uncle wanted to see Delaunay's newest pictures. The sight of the window paintings produced an outburst of fury in him; above all, he was indignant that his nephew wanted to "renew" painting. They had a serious quarrel. Later, Charles Damour struck his nephew from his will.

In Paris, the Marcs and Mackes awaited Delaunay. On October 2, they came to see him at his studio on the Rue des Grands Augustins. There seems to have been immediate and superb artistic and human rapport among the three men. Marc and Macke were wildly enthusiastic about the pictures. Delaunay, who still smarted under his uncle's reproaches, regained his equilibrium through the spontaneous, youthful admiration of the two Germans. The visit was repeated. And when Macke and Marc left, they parted from Delaunay in a spirit of friendly attachment. The letters they exchanged afterward sound like continuations of studio conversations among friends. The letters of Franz Marc, who spoke and wrote French extremely well, have been preserved. But according to Sonia Delaunay's recollection, it was the young August Macke with his winning charm and his spontaneous enthusiasm who became especially dear to Delaunay, although his French was less accomplished. After his return to Germany, Macke wrote, "Delaunay is a delightful man."[47]

Delaunay's window pictures greatly influenced Macke's and Marc's art, though in different ways and to different degrees. Every artist speaks his own language, and Marc and Macke undoubtedly used the stimulus received from Delaunay in ways that fitted in with their respective artistic intentions. But the connection between color and light, so important to Delaunay himself, meant more to Macke than it did to Marc. While Macke wrote of the window pictures, ". . . they are not abstract at all; they are of supreme reality, I see that quite clearly . . . ," Marc's letter to Kandinsky after the same visit says in part, ". . . he is working his way toward truly constructive pictures without any representation of objects; one might say: pure tonal fugues." Macke's enthusiasm was boundless, Marc's judgment cooler and more reserved: ". . . it seems to me that he still relies much too much on complementary colors and prism effects; but his things are definitely talented, and [he] is full of great intentions."[48]

Macke's strong, sensuous feeling for the vitality of color established his rapport with Delaunay. Besides, he was bound to be more open to Delaunay's influence than Marc, who was older and who had already found himself. In Marc's work of 1913–14, though, we do see traces of the window pictures – in the crystalline spaciousness of juxtaposed and superimposed color zones whose poetic transparency and depth form a medium in which the mythic essence of his animals finds a magical, cosmic connection. If we bear in mind that Marc's deepest purpose was the visualization of this cosmic relatedness, the pure harmony of all living

with the dynamics of real life. Delaunay must have seen a certain confirmation of his own ideas in this. The work produced by members of the Section d'Or has been described by Dorival: "This was a very different art from the Cubism of Braques and Picasso, in one respect much more conservative, in another much newer. It was much closer to pre-Cubism, with an emphasis on Cézanne which the artists of the Bateau Lavoir had dropped. But it also strove much more emphatically toward pure painting; it showed a drive toward abstraction."[53]

Nevertheless, the Section d'Or exhibition which took place in October of 1912 in the hall of a furniture store on the Rue La Boétie showed profound variations. These variations were so far-reaching that Apollinaire, who had of course been present at the founding of the Section d'Or and who had his own art-politics ax to grind, was hard put to fit all this diversity into a single box. He wanted to create a solid front against the continuing attacks from the press and from the general public. All artists who strove for the new were to be united under the flag of Cubism. Thus, he wrote in the first and only issue of the magazine *Section d'Or*, which appeared on October 9: "Some young people, art critics, painters, and poets, have formed an alliance in order to defend their artistic ideas – that is in itself an ideal. . . . The Cubists, no matter to which faction they belong, appear to all of us who are concerned with the future of art to be the most serious and interesting artists of our time."[54]

Delaunay did not take part in the Section d'Or exhibition; this new alliance did not mean much to him. He lived far too exclusively in his own world and was much too self-willed to let himself be placed in any group. Besides, he had not much use for art politics. But above all, he felt much closer to poets and writers than to other painters. His friendship with Apollinaire was at its most intense and mutually productive during those months.

The great Eiffel Tower pictures had demonstrated their inspiring effect on the poetry of their time. The same thing happened – but in a much more intimate sense – with the window series. One reason for this was no doubt Delaunay's personal friendship with Apollinaire and later with Blaise Cendrars. The deeper reason lay in the fact that poetry, too, was turning toward rhythm and sound as autonomous, abstract elements of decisive poetic expression, which in turn – and again by means of abstraction – assumed general validity.

Only through this constellation can we properly understand the frequently used word *poesy* in the language of the time. It did not refer to poetry alone but to the creative element in all art. Poesy was a state to which the painter was subject as much as the poet. "The poetic life inherent in matter is transmitted by matter itself: color."[55] Both realms throbbed with the same pulse, were permeated by the same passion for the rhythms of modern life. Painting could be poetic, poetry colorful and visual – a genuine simultaneity in which the two art forms merged into a single whole through mutual inspiration and influence.

Apollinaire, still suffering from the consequences of the *Mona Lisa* scandal and deeply depressed by his recent separation from Marie Laurencin, his friend of many years, spent about six weeks with the Delaunays in November and December, 1912. "Robert Delaunay's dynamism, his burning eagerness . . . had a salutary effect on Apollinaire. Their discussions distracted him from his grief and gave him back his will to work. Sonia Delaunay's friendly sympathy was a great comfort to him – he appreciated feminine attention more than anything."[56] To this must be added the pleasures of the Delaunay cuisine, to which Apollinaire was especially susceptible.

It was during these weeks that Apollinaire wrote his famous poem "Les Fenêtres." It is dedicated to Delaunay, and was first printed in 1913 by André Marty in the catalog for Delaunay's exhibit at the gallery of the Berlin magazine *Der Sturm* in January–February, 1913 (see p. 48). "Without boasting," Delaunay commented later, "I think I can say that the *Windows* had a great – I don't want to say descriptive – influence on a certain part of his poetry during that period."[57]

In this time of mutual inspiration and revelation, they were intoxicated with creativity. They did not merely produce art; they lived it. All the artistic documents of that period – Delaunay's paintings, Apollinaire's poems, and even the colorful abstract collage book covers which Sonia produced in creative concurrence – can only be understood in the light of this over-all atmosphere of genuine simultaneity.

It was the limitless depth of the window pictures, produced with color alone, and the lyrical totality of their colors which made Apollinaire coin the term *Orphism* or *Orphic Cubism*. (The words came naturally to one who, two years earlier, had completed a poetry cycle called *Orpheus' Funeral*, which was later published with illustrations by Raoul Dufy.) The name is poetic: "Here is where inspiration begins. We are on the way to a definite lyricism."[58] In his *Aesthetic Meditations*, he defines this art as

. . . a way of painting new ensembles with elements that are not borrowed from visual reality. The artist creates them completely new and gives them a powerful reality of their own. The works of the Orphic painter are to be compositions that please the aesthetic sense, and at the same time they must offer a lofty meaning, one might say: as subject matter. This is pure art.[59]

With the *Orphic Cubism*, Apollinaire also tried to place Delaunay's art within the general framework of Cubism. His art-politics goal was to unite all the younger artists, painters, and poets in a common front whose title and password was to be "Cubism." But because he had to differentiate among so many contradictory theses and trends, he was forced to introduce subdivisions into the somewhat questionable over-all idea of Cubism. Delaunay himself felt that the name *Orphism* was too literary. In his essay "Orphism," written in 1924, he said:

> Thus when Apollinaire saw an art of color emerge whose entire significance he might perhaps not have grasped, he assimilated it into the workings of poetry – in the musical and pictorial sense – and also into fantasy itself, which made so deep an impression on him. But he as a poet could perhaps not comprehend the important structural meaning. He gave the name *Orphism* to all those color statements that represented the first hope of transformation in the midst of Cubism. . . .[60]

Besides Delaunay and his wife, Sonia Terk, Maurice Raynal counted among the members of the Orphist group the Americans Patrick Henry Bruce, Morgan Russell, and Stanton MacDonald-Wright and the Czech-born Frank Kupka.[61] While the three Americans came to their color compositions directly through Delaunay's influence, Kupka's paintings originated in independent and totally different assumptions. In his "Modern Painting," written in 1912, Apollinaire added a whole string of French and foreign painters to the Orphist ranks, basing his decision only on their color palette; and he added a number of poets as well.

Whether we interpret the idea of Cubism in a narrow or in a much larger sense, it is certainly obvious that Apollinaire's efforts to interpret Delaunay's painting as a colorful version of the Cubist system rest on a misunderstanding of Delaunay's basic idea. Of course, we must consider how confusing and difficult it must have been for a contemporary to survey the wealth of competing new trends in the years 1908–14, and how strong the temptation to continue classifying Delaunay as a Cubist, since public opinion counted him among Cubism's main supporters and he had produced a major Cubist work – *The City of Paris* (plate 5) – as recently as 1912. Delaunay himself, whose intuition outstripped his ability to present it in comprehensible words, was bound to remain misunderstood, because he pursued problems which had no reality at all for the thinking of that period. Life can never recognize itself; even a towering intellect like Apollinaire could not possibly see that Delaunay's painterly thinking, as manifested in his window pictures, could not be equated or compared with anything else that existed at the time.

This was the realization that light, in its constant movement and change, produces color shapes that are independent of the presence of any object whatever, and that a certain combination of colors, in harmonic contrast with each other, can reproduce this movement of light. Thus he took the first step toward a modern representation of the universe – with purely painterly material methods that have nothing descriptive, literary, or symbolic about them.

The document in which Delaunay summarizes his ideas in the most intense and precise way is his essay "Light," which he wrote in La Madeleine and which was published in *Der Sturm* of January, 1913, in a free translation by Paul Klee. This essay stands not only on the strength of its ideas but also on the rhythm of its condensed phrases, which show Delaunay's affinity to the poetic language of his time. The visual form of the original manuscript (see pp. 6–7), with its indented lines and underlined words, also recalls the poetry of those years. It seems that Klee found the translation not easy; Delaunay's illegible handwriting gave him trouble, too: "I received your second manuscript, but before I can read it, it must be deciphered. I have made thirteen notes, and would ask you to write these thirteen words more clearly."[62] Delaunay's text, of central importance for the history of modern art, serves as an introduction to this book.

Delaunay's success at the first Blaue Reiter exhibition was to continue. In the fall of 1912, Franz Marc wrote to him that Herwarth Walden wanted to show a fairly big collective show of his work at *Der Sturm* in Berlin. Delaunay agreed with pleasure. He had a large catalog made in Paris containing the first published version of Apollinaire's "Les Fenêtres," ten reproductions, and one colorplate. He sent nineteen paintings, of which twelve were Window pictures. The show opened in the middle of January, 1913, in the exhibition room of *Der Sturm*, at 51 Königin-Augusta-Strasse. In the preliminary correspondence, Delaunay had expressed a wish that Apollinaire speak at the show. On January 13 they traveled to Berlin together, and on January 18 Apollinaire gave his lecture "Modern Painting," which he had written during his stay at the Delaunays'. A German translation was published the following month in *Der Sturm*.[63]

No definite details are known about Delaunay's stay in Berlin and the success of the exhibit, but he appears to have been very warmly received. He seems to have felt thoroughly at home in Berlin:

> I have a very good recollection of your pictures and those of your friends [he wrote to Marc]. The group of young painters I saw has given me beautiful confidence – a beautiful start toward true painting; and I saw no exception in this respect. The enthusiasm for life, light, color – these are the simultaneous impressions I have retained and which have given me confidence.... In Berlin, I did not feel like a foreigner, except for the language.... Berlin is luminous![64]

On their way back to Paris, Delaunay and Apollinaire stopped over in Bonn on January 21 in order to visit Macke. For Apollinaire, this excursion meant a trip into the past: in 1901-2, he had spent a year as a tutor with a rich German family in the Rhineland, mainly in Honnef. Apollinaire's eloquence during the visit evidently left a deep impression on everyone.

The young Max Ernst, who happened to drop in on Macke while the travelers were there, could only listen in mute admiration as Apollinaire "talked of Cubists, of Le Douanier Rousseau – about whom he and Delaunay made a big fuss – of ancient lyric poetry, of dissolute philosophers, Symbolism, aviation, and streets. 'We

were silent, overwhelmed by those winged words that swung from the lightest of subjects to the most profound, from deep emotion to laughter, from paradox to biting criticism....'"[65]

From Berlin, the Delaunay exhibition went to the Gereonsklub in Cologne, after Walden had taken out a few pictures for an exhibition in Budapest. On suggestion of Macke, who visited the Cologne show several times, Köhler bought a window picture and a small window study, both of which perished by fire in Berlin in 1945.

In December, 1912, Delaunay had answered an invitation of Franz Marc's to visit him in Munich during his trip to Berlin: "Perhaps I'll come, perhaps I won't, but I am very eager to see a collection of your pictures at your studio. As I mentioned in my last post card, I have begun two large pictures which occupy me completely, and this great work makes it impossible for me to make any arrangements in advance."[66]

One of these pictures must have been the large version of *The Three Windows, the Tower, and the Ferris Wheel* (fig. 21); the other was possibly the first version of *The Cardiff Team* (plate 14), which initiated a great new series extending to the year 1924. This first version, which is at the Stedelijk van Abbemuseum in Eindhoven today, was shown in the *Der Sturm* exhibition of January, 1913.

The Cardiff Team, a lightning flash of a scene from a soccer game, unites the presentation of human action with the giant ferris wheel, the Eiffel Tower, an airplane, and an advertising poster: elements of sport, of technical achievements – of modern life. It is Delaunay's first picture in which lettering appears as a constructive and suggestive component: ASTRA (the name of an airplane company), whose verbal sound here stands for the universe; MAGIC, standing for fascination; CONSTRUCTION, standing for the artist's program. In its large format and axial color zones and in certain thematic material the picture is related to *The Three Windows*, but there are new elements, too: the visible motion of the players, the ball, and the airplane. The motion of light forms worked out in the Window pictures now encompasses the motion of leaping player and airplane, and blends the entire ensemble into one great spatial movement: in the concurrence of its themes, a simultaneity of modern life – a single moment in the clash of various subjects and things. The space-shaping power of the large, rectangular color zones and the soft color contrasts result in a depth of strong, atmospheric vibrations.

As happens so often with Delaunay even in his verbal formulations, this first version, in its spontaneity and

Football [Soccer] 1922

freshness of ideas, is especially rich in magical color harmonies.

Among the papers kept by Sonia Delaunay, there is an interesting document – a picture torn from an illustrated newspaper which must have prompted this theme (see p. 108). The photograph shows a group of soccer players. In the center of the group one man is in the air, leaping for the ball. Delaunay incorporated this group, whose concerted motion fascinated him, into the composition of his pictures. The worn, ragged newspaper picture still shows the pencil marks with which he sketched in the giant ferris wheel as an element of his composition.

After his return from Berlin, Delaunay immediately began another version, more than ten feet high (fig. 67),

his *Troisième représentation*, which is today at the Musée du Petit Palais in Paris. Several sketches in various techniques preceded it. This picture, which he himself thought very highly of, is flatter and more severe than the earlier version; its color contrasts are sharper, more accentuated; the details are more severely defined. Where the first version is deep and shimmering, this one stresses the structural values based on pure simultaneous contrasts. This lends a feeling of sinewy and precise strength to the picture. The color planes, rigidly defined and separated, admit of no atmospheric depth; the integration of lettering, figures, and technical and sport elements produces instead the impression of a brilliantly conceived poster wall.

This picture was Delaunay's contribution to the Salon des Indépendants which opened on March 19, 1913. Apollinaire's review in *Montjoie!* of March 18 said:

With this latest picture, Delaunay has taken another step forward. His art, which used to seem intellectual – to the delight of the German university professors – now has achieved a great popular character. I think this is the greatest compliment one can pay a painter nowadays. *The Cardiff Team* . . . by Delaunay is the most modern picture at the Salon. There is nothing successive about this painting. The complementary contrasts discovered by Seurat vibrate in it, but beyond this, every color tone evokes and illuminates all the other colors of the prism. This is simultaneity – suggestive, not objective, painting – and its effect is similar to that of nature and poetry: light is the total reality here. This is the new tendency of Cubism, and we find this tendency toward Orphism in almost every picture in the adjoining room of the Salon.[67]

The lettering in the picture has undergone a transformation. Instead of MAGIC and PARIS, Delaunay has projected his own name in large letters onto the picture, followed by the words NEW YORK — PARIS. This inclusion of the American metropolis probably refers not only to Delaunay's characteristic yearning to be involved with the entire world but also to his participation in the famous Armory Show in New York, February 17–March 15, 1913. Delaunay chose one window picture, one Laon picture, and his big *City of Paris* for this first massive showing of modern art in America.

The invitation to show at the Armory, which he received with tremendous enthusiasm, ended in disappointment. The major work he sent, his *City of Paris* (plate 5), was not hung, because of its size. His old friend Sam Halpert wrote from New York, describing his futile efforts to secure a place for the picture and his indignation over the spirit of the entire organization.

Whereupon Delaunay withdrew his other pictures as well. The magazine *Montjoie!* expressed the opinion that the young French painters had only been invited as a trick, to lure the American public to the show. Actually, the article said, the exhibition showed mostly the work of Americans – French works were relegated to unfavorable locations. These remarks created bad blood on the other side of the Atlantic. The Americans replied in a long interview article.

Delaunay sent photographs of his large *Team* to his German friends Macke and Marc. Macke replied, "The photograph of your new picture has given me much pleasure. I had it hanging on the wall of our room for a long time."[68] Franz Marc was disappointed by this new step:

> If this is one of your most recent pictures, then I must confess that I expected a development diametrically opposed to its style. This is actually the sheerest Impressionism, instantaneous, photographic motion. . . . The only thing that struck me about the picture is that it is very Parisian, very French, but very far removed from my ideas. The picture I saw in your studio last fall, the long picture with the tripartite view, excited me much more.[69]

To which Delaunay replied in his typical overly emphatic way, "With this picture, which is the most perfect and beautiful subject, I have outdone myself. . . . It is the most important, the very newest picture theme in my art and at the same time the most representative in its execution."[70]

Marc's letter shows that he did not understand the picture's main point – the simultaneous action of color and body motion in a single, comprehensive construction – and it is to be presumed that neither Delaunay's self-promoting remarks nor his subsequent explanations were able to convince him. This was not the first argument by letter the two artists had engaged in. Some time earlier, Delaunay's article "Light" had given rise to a long discussion of artistic principles between them. Delaunay's vocabulary had remained incomprehensible to Marc: "*I love your pictures*, but I don't think that your philosophical and historical ideas are sound and necessary for your own artistic development or for that of others . . . certainly never for mine."[71] Delaunay's established theses, which centered around concepts like *movement, the simultaneous, the universe, and depth* in a hermetic circle, accessible only to those who were familiar with the growth of his ideas, seemed to Marc a "juggling with fine words." Delaunay's answer:

> I find myself saddened, after reading your letter, that you have understood absolutely nothing of what I said about my work and of my explanations about

Football [Soccer] (Study) 1924

the personal methods of métier in addition to the pictures. . . . You conduct philosophical meditations about questions of métier. You say you love my works. My works are the result of my striving in this métier. . . . All this is closely interrelated. How then can one understand or love one part of such a synthesis without the other part that corresponds with it?[72]

On the other hand, Marc's ideas, which aimed at a new mystic religiosity, were completely foreign to Delaunay, who wrote Marc: "For art, for progress in art, I find that no mysticism is needed, not Christian nor Jewish nor any other kind of mysticism. What makes my art different from the few things I saw in your country is this enthusiasm or rather mystic daze to which the young Germans, even the most interesting ones, are subject, and which hampers and paralyzes the vital impulse."[73]

It was a clash between two completely different worlds. And yet their letters, with all their ruthless honesty – the kind that is possible only between good friends – bear witness to a mutual liking, respect, and artistic understanding which transcended the barrier that separated them.

In November, 1912, Delaunay had met Blaise Cendrars for the first time at Apollinaire's apartment.

Cendrars was then a young, little-known modern poet. He was still testing his powerful, robust, vivid, and contemporaneous poetic language. He was an inveterate traveler who had wandered all over the world since childhood. He had worked at the most adventurous jobs; he had crossed the Orient buying and selling pearls and searching for diamonds, and had got as far as China. He had studied medicine in Bern and later tried his luck at raising bees in Paris. He had appeared as a juggler in a London music hall along with Charlie Chaplin, spent some time in Moscow, traveled through all of Russia to Siberia, and later come to North America, where he had worked on a farm in Canada. At Easter, 1912, wandering hungry and in rags through the streets of New York, he wrote his famous poem "Les Pâques" – "Easter." That fall, he returned to Paris.

Life and poetry were one and the same to Cendrars. "To be a poet is to live as intensely as possible, to use, even to misuse, the feverish activity of modern life."[74] This young poet, who had seen the whole world by the time he was twenty-five, who wrote in an unsentimental, forceful, and direct – altogether modern – poetic language, truly had lived his work. His poetry evoked images, suggested motor noises, smells, speed, ideas, and experiences – all dimensions of reality simultaneously, in one breath, experiences of contemporary reality gathered on three continents.

"Apollinaire's and Cendrars' art are completely different," said Delaunay. "Apollinaire is sensitive, always in search of new spiritual values. . . . Cendrars belongs to the younger generation, which is new in itself."[75] And elsewhere: "Cendrars was more direct, graphic. He compared the simultaneous with reinforced concrete. This means a large view of the future."[76] Cendrars was enthusiastic about Delaunay's Eiffel Towers, whose dramatic quality gave him a sense of relatedness: he dedicated a poem to them. In the two years that followed, his poems accompanied the works of Delaunay – verbal equivalents of his color-shape inventions of contrasts, fed by the same sense of life.

In January, 1913, Cendrars made Sonia a present of his "Easter" manuscript. She was delighted; in a state of productive excitement created by the poem, she bound the notebook in leather the next day and decorated the cover and end papers with vividly rhythmic abstract color collages. This first bookbinding achievement was followed by others, always of poetry, which she loved and which put her in a creative mood.

Her cover for "Easter" gave rise to the idea that this combination of poetry and color creation could be extended to the color-rhythmic accompaniment of an entire poem. Thus, February of 1913 saw the creation of a unique document of the period, the "simultaneous book" *La Prose du Transsibérien et la petite Joanne de France – The Sequence [Hymn] of the Trans-Siberian and Little Joanne of France*. This poem by Cendrars is an internal monolog of the poet aboard the Trans-Siberian Express. Remembered images combine and contrast with immediate impressions of surroundings and imagined creations in a time continuum. The format of the book corresponds with this unfolding process; about fourteen inches wide, it opens out to a length of some six and a half feet. The painting accompanies the poem along its full length like a rhythmic-coloristic score, painted in a state of poetic unanimity.

Cendrars, who had never had any money, came into a small inheritance just then. He used it up completely to get the book in print. It was brought out in an edition of 150 copies by Les Hommes Nouveaux, printed in letters of different sizes and colors; Sonia's abstract color composition, along the left margin to the full height of the text, unfolds with the poem. The book, today a bibliophilic rarity of the first rank, created an international sensation when it appeared, and gave rise to literary controversies in newspapers and magazines in Paris and outside France. It was exhibited in Paris, New York, Saint Petersburg, Moscow, Berlin, London, and elsewhere. The original pictorial design by Sonia Delaunay is today at the Musée National d'Art Moderne.

The joint creative work deepened their friendship. Cendrars came almost daily to the Delaunays', where an ever larger circle was beginning to form. Acquaintance and friendship with many new people – the young Chagall, the painters Jacouloff, Rossiné, the Americans Bruce and Frost, the Swiss Alice Bailly, and others – made life varied and vivid. Every Thursday, the entire company went to the Bal Bullier at the top of the Boulevard Saint-Michel opposite the Closerie des Lilas. In a colorful carnival atmosphere, the avant-garde artists mingled with the people and danced through the night with the midinettes of Paris. But Delaunay and Apolli-

once called this experiment a "blow with a fist." Round about, always in circular forms, I placed other contrasts, always juxtaposed to each other, always simultaneous in respect to the picture as a whole, that is, to the totality of its colors. . . . The experiment was striking. No more bowls of fruit, no Eiffel Towers, no streets, no landscape; but they thought I was crazy, my friends looked at me askance. I might well shout: "I've found it. It rotates!" They turned away from me. . . .

This is the cosmic, visible, truly real form![79]

The disc of which Delaunay speaks here is a circular picture which probably dates back to November–December, 1912 (fig. 23). It is a disc divided into four segments with concentrically placed color zones.

Delaunay did not show this first disc painting at any of the representative shows outside France during 1913, nor did he show it at the Indépendants' exhibitions of 1913 and 1914. Its first public presentation took place in 1922. This makes it safe to assume that he himself considered the piece a private experiment. Only later, when viewed in retrospect, did it assume documentary importance as his first abstract painting. Unquestionably, it must be counted among the incunabula of nonobjective painting, and Delaunay's subsequent abstract work is based on the fundamental formula he discovered with this picture. From 1912 to 1920, the importance of the disc for Delaunay lay in its completely nonobjective appearance. This was different from the window pictures: " . . . no longer analysis, description, psychology, but the purely pictorial form whose color relations are its building blocks."[80] This was also Delaunay's view of the substantially new.

In order to understand this first circular form, we must remember that it was created during those same months when Delaunay's thinking and painting were most intensely concentrated on the essence of light, the "sole reality."[81] Movement, implying the life of light, had been confined to certain axes – horizontal, vertical, or diagonal, and radiating toward infinity – in his window pictures. Delaunay must have striven to find a viable basic model that would contain the totality of colors and given a form both infinite and self-contained to the motion of light. "A painting created according to the laws of this organization is a small universe in tune with the rhythm of the cosmos."[82] In this sense, the disc was for Delaunay a total mobile form. Equivalent to the whole of reality, it was for him the cell from which he could derive the representation of the macrocosm (sun, moon) and a new structure for presenting small, individual incidents (still life). The boundaries of representation had been widened to include

the viewer's emotion when faced with the light-filled cosmos, and to blend this emotion into the object.

Everyone's eyes are sensitive to color and to the wave play and vibrations, rhythms, counterpoints, fugues, depths, variations, harmonious chords, monumental ensembles of these colors. This signifies architecture. By which I mean a certain kind of order. Not an artificial order but a construction that corresponds with our sense of proportion, man's feeling for proportion. . . . It is the heartbeat of active, living man.[83]

For Delaunay, the movement created by color contrasts was an abbreviation of the world; it was the basic structure combining every living thing with the motion of light. Thus, the invention of the circular form did not mean an alternative for him between "abstract" and "representational" painting. On the contrary, the construction he had realized from purely creative means made it possible for him to cancel this contradistinction; it gave him freedom in all directions. After the vertical and horizontal color contrasts of the window pictures comes a period of discs and suns, his so-called *époque circulaire*, or circle period.

In April, 1913, the Delaunays and some of their friends rented a house near the Château Louveciennes, west of Paris. They stayed there until November. They were close enough to Paris to prevent a complete break with the city, and now the whole circle of friends often met in Louveciennes. They continued to visit the Bal Bullier, frequently returning late at night with a crowd of friends and acquaintances who were given improvised sleeping facilities throughout the house, sometimes even on the billiard table.

During those months in Louveciennes, Delaunay painted his *formes circulaires*, his circular forms, suns and moons (plates 11, 12; figs. 24–27, 60, 61). This is again a series. He finished it in a way in 1913, but toward 1930 he took it up again under different conditions in monumental wall pictures (figs. 28, 29).

It is possible that Delaunay, completely absorbed by the universal creative possibilities which the invention of his disc promised, chose Louveciennes for the added reason that he could pursue his grand visions better outside the city. Sonia Delaunay reports that he spent much time observing the emanations of the sun and the moon, their light effects and zones of brightness in the clouds. "I am in the country now, and working a great deal," he wrote to Macke on June 2; "my last picture is the *sun*. It shines more and more brightly the more I work on it. From now on, all my new synchromies will be born out of this motion. The window pictures marked their beginning."[84]

In his series of Sun and Moon pictures, Delaunay tried for the first time to test the validity of his basic findings through circular forms against reality. The reality he meant is that of the sun's and moon's light in its differentiation. No images of the heavenly bodies in any descriptive sense appear on these canvases; Delaunay strove to constitute specific kinds of light by means of color shapes. If we consider this pictorial idea within the frame of the artistic development of that time, we recognize that it is unique; here is a method of developing pure painting in strict conjunction with an objectively given reality.

In Delaunay's conception, light is actualized through color. The more intense the light, the more active must the colors be. But any color taken by itself is merely an amorphous entity; only in juxtaposition to a contrasting or related color can it attain expression, intensity, and movement. With a contrasting color, there is intensification; with a related color, there is dissonance. But this reaction can be accomplished according to the rules only when the contiguous colors retain certain proportions which determine the form. Thus, form is born out of color and is identical to it.

The development of these rules was possible only with as abstract a subject as the creation of light. To represent the most intense light – the light of the sun – colors had to be intensified and activated to the dazzling point by means of complementary and light-dark contrasts, whereas the moon sphere retained gliding color passages. But complementary and dissonant contrasts produce movement physically perceptible to the eye: complementary contrasts produce slow vibrations, dissonant contrasts fast. These vibrations, generated by simultaneous contrasts, are what Delaunay meant when he spoke of movement: neither successive nor descriptive, but continuous and therefore truly real movement. Through observation of these slow and fast movements of contrasts, he developed the principle of all his later color constructions; it is the theoretical foundation of his new creative material, in whose attainment lies the developmental importance of his suns and moons.

This does not mean that Delaunay applied these systematic perceptions in an intellectual or dogmatic way. They are part of his métier, of the means he needed in order to give form to his powerful poetic vision in ultimate purity – to execute structures that had long been inherent in his artistic volition. We can see them as early as 1906 in his *Landscape with Disc* (fig. 5), in the pen-and-ink drawings of the Eiffel Tower, and in the football flying toward the light in his first *Cardiff Team* (plate 14). They become more and more precise until

they achieve their final incarnation in the *Circular Forms (Moon) No. 2* of 1913 (fig. 26).

Thus in 1912, the year of his discoveries about light and of his window pictures, Delaunay made the fundamental invention which enabled him to push back the boundaries of what had been depictable heretofore to include the kind of totality contained in the circular form. To the world which in his Eiffel Towers was still confined to human communications around the terrestrial globe, he had now added the universe.

The series of suns and moons consists of two groups: about nine small pictures, some of them mere studies, in which the sun and moon appear separately; and three large pictures in which the two light systems are united in mutual tension on a single canvas. Today, various of these pictures are at the Museum of Modern Art in New York, the Stedelijk Museum in Amsterdam (plate 11), and the Kunsthaus in Zurich. The Zurich picture, which is dated 1912–31, was presumably begun at an early date, may have been repeatedly painted over, and did not get its final form until 1931. The first date, 1912, probably designates the year of its initial conception, as many of Delaunay's datings do.

The series of small suns (among them figs. 24, 60) shows the way Delaunay proceeded from comparatively rigid schemes, in which circular forms and axial cross stand in static relation to each other, to a more and more dramatic expression by intensifying his contrasts, mutually interchanging his forms, and increasingly interpenetrating the two systems. The light structure takes on movement, becoming an active element of extreme radiance and color exaltation.

The floating light sphere of the moon (fig. 27), however, was shaped into a form motif of supreme simplicity by Delaunay: two dark ovals on a slanting axis hold between them, with the most delicate touch, an oval light form shrouded in circular color zones of pearly, iridescent blue, green, pink, and violet – chromatic passages whose mystical poetry rests on the rapport of related colors that are graded against each other by intensity and brightness.

Delaunay's vision encompassed the realization of painting itself by the representation of these two color worlds and their specific color systems. "At this moment I am painting the sun, which is nothing else but – painting itself."[85]

If we regard the development from the *City* of December, 1911, through the windows and discs to the three great sun-moon pictures as the gradual building up of a great systematic thought structure, we might say that these three pictures represent its temporary

The opening, on September 20, 1913, had all the earmarks of a demonstration. Robert and Sonia Delaunay, who had brought along their little son, met many of their German and Parisian friends there: Marc, Macke, Arp, Chagall, and Cendrars. The last spoke at the exhibition on September 29. His talk, in German, was on "Today, the Spirit of the New Man."

The most exciting aspect of this show – apart from Chagall's first appearance in Germany – was the presence of works by both Delaunay and the Italian Futurists. Since Delaunay and the Futurists used the same words, *movement* and *simultaneity*, as slogans for their work, there were bound to be complications and controversy. It began with Apollinaire's writing that Delaunay had borrowed the term *simultaneous* from the vocabulary of the Futurists.[89] Umberto Boccioni, the spokesman for the Futurists, immediately picked up this remark in order to prove the Futurists' influence on French artists, especially Delaunay.[90] He referred emphatically to the testimony of "our friend and ally, Apollinaire." In the same article, he claimed priority for the first simultaneous sculpture for himself. This brought a reply from Apollinaire, who considered himself the father of the idea of simultaneous sculpture. He stated that he had discussed the idea with several artist friends, including Delaunay, Raymond Duchamp-Villon and his brother Marcel Duchamp, Gleizes, and Léger, as early as the spring of 1913 – long before Boccioni's show in Paris. In the same article, Apollinaire disputed any direct influence of the Futurists on French painting, and closed with the remark: "But the Futurists have not found anyone here who would follow them, and their method of painting swift motion has remained stationary in the country where it was born."[91] Two days after this article appeared, Delaunay sent an open letter to *Der Sturm* in which he brilliantly countered Boccioni's attack with quotes from Apollinaire.[92]

But a few months later, Apollinaire, his own earlier remarks notwithstanding, characterized Delaunay's large *Homage to Blériot* (plate 13) as "rotating Futurism" when it was shown at the Indépendants in March, 1914 (*L'Intransigeant* of March 4, 1914). This drew an immediate, sharply worded reply from Delaunay which appeared in *L'Intransigeant* the next day, March 5:

Sir,

Permit me to appeal to your kind impartiality with respect to a criticism by Mr. Guillaume Apollinaire which is more personal than artistic and in which he sets himself up as the apostle of the Futurists in France, whereas all French artists have considered Futurism merely a foreign trend in which they are not interested.

But I will not permit a critic, who should be better informed, after all, to commit such an error at my expense, an error that paves the way for intolerable misconceptions. I am not and I never was a Futurist; no critic could ever have any doubt in this regard. I am amazed at Mr. Apollinaire's ignorance of the simultaneous contrasts which make up the construction and the novelty of my work.

Thus, the controversy over Futurism led to a personal quarrel. There had been a certain estrangement between Delaunay and Apollinaire earlier on. It dated back to Delaunay's acquaintance and growing friendship with Cendrars. The rivalry between the two poets may well have played a part in it – Apollinaire's sensitive ego was hurt. He was used to being the center of admiration. Besides, by 1913 his interest had begun to shift toward the circle around the editorial offices of the magazine *Les Soirées de Paris*, whose editor-in-chief he was. The center of this group was the Baroness d'Oettingen, who with her brother Serge Férat (Jastrebzoff) financed the magazine. Picasso, Léger, Ossip Zadkine, Raynal, Max Jacob, Giorgio de Chirico, and the Italian Futurists Gino Severini and Ardengo Soffici were constant visitors.

Apart from this personal controversy, the idea that Delaunay was influenced by Futurism has carried over almost into the present. This idea is erroneous: for Delaunay, movement never meant a displacement in the sense of an object changing its place in space, as it did for the Futurists, but always referred to the movement of light and simultaneous color contrasts:

In the movement of colors, there are varying values of speed:
the *slow* movement of complementary colors, and
the *fast* movement of dissonant colors.
This has nothing to do with the *descriptive* motion of the Cubist-Futurists, which the painters call *dynamism*. The movements I mean – I experience them vividly; *I do not describe them*. Through their contrasts, they are simultaneous – not successive.[93]

In short, Delaunay's concept of simultaneity was different from that of the Futurists. In the spring of 1912, when the Futurist show took place in Paris, Delaunay was painting his window pictures, the first manifestations of his simultaneous contrasts; that same year he wrote a letter to Kandinsky which shows he did not foresee a long life expectancy for the Futurists – despite their success – because in his opinion they did not have the true method.[94]

The sun and moon pictures are important in Delaunay's development because they were the theme through which he perfected his system of pure painting. At the same time and later, he completed a group of pictures which show that his thinking at that moment was dominated not by the idea of abstraction but by that of construction. In this thinking, as noted earlier, there was no contradiction between abstract and objective elements since the intensity of his research was aimed mainly at refining new *methods* for the definition of reality.

In the series of the great Eiffel Towers of 1910, Delaunay had concentrated on the dramatic contest between light and object: light had destroyed the object's outline and thus the object itself. When he came back to the subject in 1913 with his picture *Sun, Tower, Airplane* (plate 10), every element of the picture became a part of a single color construction – the abstract shape of the sunlight as well as the objective shapes of the Tower, the airplane, and the giant ferris wheel. In the entire ensemble, light forms an independent "figure" which is intensified into a kind of colored euphoria but does *not* fragmentize the objective elements; the dramatic quality of the action remains self-related.

But Delaunay's intention was above all to combine the system of his circular forms with reality, and to make it ever richer and more flexible by testing its application in ever newer experiments. In the motif of the *Rainbow* (fig. 62), he found his theory confirmed by a natural shape. But his strongest impulse came from electric light, which was just beginning to transform nocturnal Paris into a sea of light globes. His striving to construct this kind of light and its vibration in color is mingled with his pride and enthusiasm over modern technical achievements. Cendrars wrote:

Il pleut des globes électriques

Montrouge Gare de l'Est Métro Nord-Sud bateaux-
    mouches monde

Tout est halo

Profoundeur. . . .

("It's raining electric light globes / Montrouge East Station Subway North-South steamers world / Everthing is a halo / Depth. . . .")

With his *Carrousel of Pigs*, Delaunay returned to a theme he had first taken up in 1906. He himself demolished the monumental picture that was shown at the Berlin Herbstsalon of 1913 (as he did the 1906 rendition); thus, we can only surmise what it was like by looking at the third version of this same theme, done in 1922 (fig. 70), which is said to be based directly on the 1913 version. In the later picture, the circular forms representing electric globes with their halos cutting across each other are the main theme of the composition. Delaunay also used these aureoles of electric light in his series of small *Simultaneous Dress* pictures (figs. 63, 64), "electric constructions" in which a figure motif – Sonia Delaunay in her simultaneous clothes – is connected to

two discs which cut across each other, rotating in opposite directions.

On March 29, 1914, the front page of *Le Petit Journal* carried an illustration of a recent political tragedy: Madame Caillaux, the wife of the French Minister of Finance, shooting down Monsieur Gaston Calmette, the editor of *Le Figaro* (see p. 108). This page, which is preserved in Delaunay's papers, was the immediate inspiration for his composition *Political Drama* (fig. 65). The picture tempted him – the idea of painting the shot directly as an explosion of light and sound. The two figures, the shooting woman and the falling man, pasted onto the disc in a form of collage, seem to be whirled around and around on the sound waves of the explosion.

The rotating motion of the electric constructions and the radial explosions of the *Political Drama* were new elements which enriched the system of circular forms with important new dimensions and decisively perfected its applicability to the construction of reality in Delaunay's sense.

Homage to Blériot (plate 13), exhibited in the spring of 1914 at the Indépendants, embraces all these elements in a grandiose composition.

The hall at the Indépendants in which the big picture (more than eight feet square) had a dominant position offered a veritable orgy of circular forms. Next to the wild turbulence of Sonia Delaunay's *Electric Prisms*, in the same monumental format, hung discs by the Orphists Bruce and Ottmann; in the next room were others by the young American Frost.

Homage to Blériot[95] is a hymn to the sun, to technical achievement, to life:

. . . fireworks of sunlight. Depth and life of the sun. Constructive mobility of the sun spectrum; beginning, flame, evolution of airplanes.

All is roundness – sun, earth, horizon, a wealth of intense life, of poetry that cannot be expressed in words. . . . The machine in the picture.

Power of sun and power of earth.[96]

Or, as Delaunay wrote elsewhere, "Analysis of the sun disc at sunset in a deep, clear sky with countless electric prisms flooding the earth, from which airplanes rise."[97]

The builder Delaunay saw the builder Blériot as his brother.

In almost deafening simultaneity, the light of the setting sun, the blinding effect of electric lights, the roar of motors, and the vibration of airplanes have been incorporated into a wealth of clear, precise, rotating color shapes. The rotation of large and small discs, cutting across each other and cut across by the aureoles of electric lights, fills almost the entire large surface. All objective elements – the airplanes, the Eiffel Tower,

28 The dating 1910–12 on *The City of Paris* (plate 5) is perhaps explained by Delaunay's frequent practice of giving a picture two dates – the year it was initially conceived and the year it was executed.

29 Delaunay, *Du Cubisme à l'art abstrait*, p. 98. Delaunay's letter quoted here was not written to Sam Halpert in 1924 but to André Lhote in 1933, in answer to an inquiry dated July 10, 1933.

30 *Ibid.*

31 *Ibid.*, p. 60.

32 See Johannes Langner, "Zu den Fenster-Bildern von Robert Delaunay," in *Jahrbuch der Hamburger Kunstsammlungen*, VII, Hamburg, 1962, 67 ff.

33 Delaunay, *Du Cubisme à l'art abstrait*, p. 110.

34 *Ibid.*, p. 113.

35 Maurice Princet, letter to Robert Delaunay whose first page is missing, 1912.

36 Guillaume Apollinaire, "Réalité: Peinture pure," quoted in Delaunay, *Du Cubisme à l'art abstrait*, pp. 154 ff.

37 Delaunay, *Du Cubisme à l'art abstrait*, p. 97.

38 According to an oral report.

39 Quoted in Gustav Vriesen, *August Macke*, Stuttgart, 1957, p. 118.

40 Quoted in Léon Degand, "R. Delaunay," *Art d'aujourd'hui*, no. 8, 1951, p. 9.

41 From the stenographic notes of a meeting, February 16, 1939; in Delaunay, *Du Cubisme à l'art abstrait*, pp. 229 ff.

42 Maurice Raynal, *Moderne Malerei*, Geneva, 1959, III, 133.

43 Quoted in Bernard Dorival, *Die französischen Maler des 20. Jahrhunderts*, Munich, 1959, I, 77.

44 Quoted in Raynal, *op. cit.*, III, 70. The pun means literally "reasoning cubery," a play on the French term *cube racine* (cube root).

45 Delaunay, *Du Cubisme à l'art abstrait*, p. 216.

46 *Ibid.*, p. 109.

47 August Macke, letter to Bernhard Köhler, October 8, 1912; quoted in Vriesen, *op. cit.*, p. 116.

48 Quoted in K. Lankheit, *Unteilbares Sein, Aquarelle und Zeichnungen von Franz Marc*, Cologne, 1959, p. 19.

49 Max Imdahl, "Die Farbe als Licht bei August Macke," in *August Macke: Gedenkausstellung zum 70. Geburtstag*, catalog of the exhibition, Landesmuseum, Münster, 1957, p. 26.

50 Paul Klee, "Die Ausstellung des 'Modernen Bundes' im Kunsthaus Zürich," *Die Alpen* (Bern), VI, no. 12, August, 1912, 700.

51 Paul Klee, *Tagebücher*, Cologne, 1957, p. 279.

52 See Gerd Henniger, "Paul Klee und Robert Delaunay," *Quadrum*, III, 1957, p. 137.

53 Dorival, *op. cit.*, p. 99.

54 Quoted in Adéma, *op. cit.*, pp. 148–49.

55 Delaunay, *Du Cubisme à l'art abstrait*, p. 173.

56 Adéma, *op. cit.*, pp. 152–53.

57 Published in *Art Documents, éléments pour l'histoire du Cubisme*, n.d. (after 1935).

58 Guillaume Apollinaire, "La Peinture moderne," quoted in Delaunay, *Du Cubisme à l'art abstrait*, p. 166.

59 Guillaume Apollinaire, *Méditations esthétiques*, quoted by Francastel, in Delaunay, *Du Cubisme à l'art abstrait*, p. 166.

60 Delaunay, *Du Cubisme à l'art abstrait*, p. 169.

61 Maurice Raynal, *De Picasso au Surréalisme*, vol. 3 of *Histoire de la peinture moderne*, Geneva, 1950, p. 90.

62 Paul Klee, letter to Robert Delaunay, December 30, 1912; in Delaunay's estate.

63 Guillaume Apollinaire, "Die moderne Malerei," tr. of "La Peinture moderne," *Der Sturm*, III, no. 148–49, February, 1913.

64 Delaunay, *Du Cubisme à l'art abstrait*, pp. 188–89.

65 P. Waldberg, *Max Ernst*, Paris, 1958, pp. 82–83.

66 Delaunay, *Du Cubisme à l'art abstrait*, p. 181.

67 Quoted in Sonia Delaunay, *op. cit.*

68 August Macke, letter to Robert Delaunay, April, 1913; in Sonia Delaunay's archives.

69 Franz Marc, letter to Robert Delaunay, April 14, 1913.

70 Robert Delaunay, letter to Franz Marc, April, 1913.

71 Franz Marc, letter to Robert Delaunay, December, 1912.

72 Delaunay, *Du Cubisme à l'art abstrait*, pp. 181–82.

73 Robert Delaunay, letter to Franz Marc, April (?), 1913.

74 Quoted in J. Rousselot, *Blaise Cendrars*, Paris, 1955, p. 58.

75 Delaunay, *Du Cubisme à l'art abstrait*, p. 111.

76 *Ibid.*, p. 172.

77 Quoted in A. Jakowsky, *Les Feux de Montparnasse*, Paris, 1957, p. 59.

78 *Blaise Cendrars vous parle*, "Entretiens de la Radiodiffusion Française" series, M. Manoll, Paris, 1952, pp. 141–42.

79 Delaunay, *Du Cubisme à l'art abstrait*, p. 217.

80 *Ibid.*, p. 98.

81 Apollinaire, "Réalité: Peinture pure," p. 155.

82 Albert Gleizes, quoted in Walter Hess, *Dokumente zum Verständnis der Modernen Malerei*, Hamburg, 1956, p. 66.

83 Delaunay, *Du Cubisme à l'art abstrait*, pp. 217 ff.

84 Robert Delaunay, letter to August Macke, June 2, 1913, written in German by Sonia Delaunay; in the Macke Archives, Bonn.

85 Robert Delaunay, letter to Franz Marc, April 17, 1913; in Delaunay, *Du Cubisme à l'art abstrait*, p. 161.

86 Nell Walden, *Der Sturm, ein Gedenkbuch an Herwarth Walden und die Künstler des Sturmkreises*, Baden-Baden, 1954, pp. 15–16.

87 Delaunay, *Du Cubisme à l'art abstrait*, p. 110.

88 *Ibid.*, p. 184.

89 Guillaume Apollinaire, in *Les Soirées de Paris*, no. 18, November 15, 1913.

90 Umberto Boccioni, "Simultanéité futuriste," *Der Sturm*, IV, no. 190–91, December, 1913.

91 Guillaume Apollinaire, in *Les Soirées de Paris*, no. 19, December 15, 1913.

92 Robert Delaunay, "Lettre ouverte au *Sturm*," December 17, 1913; *Der Sturm*, IV, no. 194–95, January, 1914.

93 Delaunay, *Du Cubisme à l'art abstrait*, p. 184.

94 See *ibid.*, p. 179.

95 Louis Blériot (1872–1936), French pilot and builder, was the first man to fly across the English Channel (July 25, 1909). Blériot himself never saw this painting, but he wrote Delaunay a few lines thanking him for the honor.

96 Delaunay, *Du Cubisme à l'art abstrait*, pp. 63–64.

97 *Ibid.*, p. 126.

98 *Ibid.*, p. 129.

99 See Hans Platte, "Robert Delaunay und Lyonel Feininger," in *Jahrbuch der Hamburger Kunstsammlungen*, III, Hamburg, 1958.

100 Delaunay, *Du Cubisme à l'art abstrait*, pp. 140–41.

Saint-Séverin 1909–10

III Max Imdahl

Delaunay's Position in History

I

For painting, light is a style-forming force. W. Schöne has described the history of painting as a history of the pictorial representation of light. He distinguished between two kinds of depicted light: inherent or "self-light," which was dominant in medieval painting; and extraneous or "illuminating light," which predominates in Renaissance and post-Renaissance pictures. We are told that in modern painting, light reaches us "only by means of substantial emanation from color," but that we are not made "aware of light as an independent factor." According to Schöne, "these messages of color" are not "messages of light."[1]

Some years earlier, H. Sedlmayr wrote an essay about the relation of art to the sun in various periods and regions and in the work of different artists. He pointed out that the sun is "the transfiguring principle of the 'golden' age of Claude Lorrain"; it can be the "universal sun mist of the 'plein-air' school of painting which transfigures all things equally, dwindling away into colored nothingness, as in the light painting of Impressionism"; and it can be "a demonic, melting ball of fire, as in Van Gogh's Expressionism."[2]

Like Schöne, Sedlmayr observed in a different place: "We might say that since Cézanne, light has become swallowed up by color, which now assumes all the power and force that once belonged to light when light was independent of color and superior to it."[3]

In French painting, the predominance of color has logically brought about an increasing concentration on the spectrum. It led first to Pointillist Impressionism and then, in Delaunay's work, where color was no longer applied in dots but spread out in planes, to non-objective painting.[4] The decisive new approach to light painting by means of the spectrum colors of Pointillism seems to aim not so much at a portrait-like representation of light – which affords the viewer a kind of contem-plative observation, as did preceding methods of depicting light – as at energizing the eye with a force that corresponds with the energy of light itself, and producing an experience of optical collaboration with light. This was also Delaunay's aim; once we understand this, we also understand the opening remark of his essay on light, the first sentence in this book: "Impressionism is the birth of *Light* in painting."[5]

Light as pure energy, as rhythm, as "rhythmic Simultaneity," as universal action, as "synchronic movement"[6] – more than any other painter in our century, Robert Delaunay valued this action that takes place in the eye, when it perceives color, as our optic share in a reality that is energized through light. Victor Vasarely nowadays says of his own work that we have changed from "static spectators" to "dynamic participants";[7] this same remark may well be applied to Delaunay's artistic intentions. It also emphasizes the revolutionary character of Pointillist Impressionism Delaunay's "pure painting," the use of color purely for the liberation and ordering of its inherent energy values, seems more closely related to the shimmering gold backgrounds of the Middle Ages than to modern representations of extraneous light, be it in sacred or profane illumination. And there is no reason that light, thus resolved into its energy values, cannot be experienced in the form of an optical as well as a spiritual reality.

Color painting can be assumed to engage the eye in two ways: below its natural adaptational limit and right up to that limit; in the first case the eye can get used to the colors effortlessly, while in the second the eye is provoked to the point of strain so that seeing becomes a conscious activity, which in turn activates the phenomenon perceived. Given this assumption, it appears that the first color use belongs to the mimetic, or portrait-like, reproductions of light, whereas the second is what we find in Delaunay's pictures: colored light equivalents. His colors correspond with light itself; they invigorate the eye as does a flash of pure light. Delaunay's pictures from 1912 to 1914 make the eye open wide; they exist in total activation of the eye through the picture – and of the picture through the eye. Nothing intervenes between eye and picture. These works are, like the light the unfolding of sight itself. In this respect, Robert Delaunay's theme was sight itself, as well as light and color.

2

Even apart from considerations of light and how to represent it, the theme of sight frequently dominates modern painting. According to José Ortega y Gasset, painters paint "first ... things, then impressions. ... At first the artist's attention turns to the outer reality, then to subjective elements." And: "Instead of painting things as one sees them, one paints sight itself."[8]

Georges Desvallières once said of the young Matisse that he was the first to liberate the eye.[9] Desvallières' words go back to 1908. Earlier still, the poet Jules Laforgue explained in a posthumously published essay that modern Impressionist painting aimed at remaking the eye into an independently active, self-motivating organ. The eye, he said, was not made for thinking but for seeing – for "pure sight," as we would say today; it should be to painting what the ear is to music. The Impressionist, gifted with an extraordinarily sensitive eye, was entirely oriented toward the new. He ignored all those paintings that had been piling up in museums for hundreds of years as completely as he ignored all academic laws of optics in order to re-create a natural eye for himself and to paint exactly what he saw without inhibition.[10] And there is Cézanne's well-known remark that Monet was all eye, but by God what an eye! Cézanne himself defined painting as a matter of visibility, for which he claimed "the logic of orderly sense impressions";[11] one is reminded of the modern concept of "inner-optical intelligence."[12]

In connection with Cézanne's pictures, Sedlmayr tried to explain so-called pure sight as a way of seeing in which the mind no longer shares the eye's experiences: "There exists a state in our normal experience, more or less corresponding with this condition, which Cézanne has stipulated as a principle. It is that state between waking up and being fully awake in which one might say that only the eye is awake while the intellect still sleeps."[13] Thus, to describe pure sight as a theme of modern painting would not necessarily be new. For instance, we might remember what John Ruskin said

about the art of William Turner around the middle of the last century. According to Ruskin, the entire power of painting consists in its restoring what he called the eye's innocence, that is, a kind of childlike receptivity to the visual as to a series of flat color patches without any knowledge of what they are meant to represent – "as if a blind man suddenly had his sight restored."[14]

But what Ruskin praised in Turner as his power of painting Sedlmayr criticized in Cézanne; he maintained that Cézanne's painting could not stand up to a critique by our "clear knowledge" or, to put it another way, to our knowledge of the objective existence of things. Kurt Badt countered this criticism emphatically. According to him, the truth in Cézanne's art lies in his presentation of an inviolably cohesive world or, conversely, in the representation of the world's cohesiveness.[15] And earlier, Rainer Maria Rilke called Cézanne's work a kind of materialization – a reality intensified to the point of indestructibility.[16] This is a materialization of purely optical phenomena, of "coloring sensations,"[17] as Cézanne himself called them. To illustrate the opposite view, one might quote the Classicist Ingres, who demanded that painters employ a linearist, sculptural method.[18]

As for German opinions, Hans von Marées, according to his pupil Karl von Pidoll, considered the artist's work a "cohesive process of development and perception" that was to "develop our ability to see and comprehend the world around us."[19] Here too the act of purely optical perception is not a precondition but the very subject of painting. The philosopher Konrad Fiedler said the same thing when he commented that painting should "show the world only in respect to visible appearances" – a representation, in other words, "created by and for the eye." And Fiedler insisted emphatically that " . . . the ability to look ought to be developed for purposes of regular and conscious use, just as the ability to think in abstract terms is consciously developed." Indeed, knowledge that comes to us via visual contemplation might, according to Fiedler, "be the true, the ultimate, the highest form of knowledge."[20]

Taking up the subject, Adolf von Hildebrand, perhaps the most important German art critic before the turn of the century, measured the beauty of the figures in Hans von Marées' paintings not by their actual proportions so much as by the architectural harmony of their optical appearance in the picture, that is, by the aesthetic pleasure they produced as a beautifully balanced two-dimensional configuration. Hildebrand's theory is concerned not with the world as such but with the world seen through men's eyes: "As in algebra, where numerical values are abstracted and value is expressed

that is played elsewhere by curtains, tree trunks, or foliage.[27] Francastel's interpretation is based on another of Delaunay's theses, that light as an element destroys the line as a constructive agent.[28] In principle, this idea of Delaunay's could be compared with something the Futurist Umberto Boccioni said in 1914 about the form-altering powers of the immaterial – that "the square of an open window," for instance, "becomes an irregular, variable body due to the currents of power that pass through it."[29] As early as 1912, Erwin von Busse said in discussing a Saint-Séverin picture that it had been Delaunay's intention "to concentrate the viewer's eye upon the center," and that this was done by means of "a spatial dynamic created by the appropriate distribution and correspondence of color, and by such curves as correspond with the tendency toward motion."[30] More recently, Georg Schmidt said that the interior was "not constructed in the sense of classical perspective from a single viewpoint, but was experienced successively by an eye moving through space in circles."[31]

Perhaps the pictures of the interior of Saint-Séverin aim at making the viewer feel inside the church. Not that this feeling would place the viewer in a definite, realistic spot that could be localized somewhere on the floor of the church interior; no, being inside as a general experience is what is suggested here. Even the space renderings of the old masters do not always presuppose the fiction that the viewer is standing on the ground level of the depicted area.

We feel extremely close to the nearest columns, no matter at what height we are viewing them. If we want to see those columns whole, they are too close to be encompassed by a single glance. It is necessary to move or shift our glance, and it is this motion that the curvature of the columns seems to describe. The columns that are farther away and can therefore be seen more easily at a single glance have correspondingly less curvature. Thus, the column standing all the way in the background seems the straightest of all. In other words, the various degrees of curvature in the columns exactly correspond with their various distances from the viewer's vantage point. In this way, they express the various viewing angles and the motion-filled viewing process the viewer himself is forced to perform at close range to the nearest columns – that is, when he himself is inside the church. The church interior as the pictorial object – what is seen in the picture – here expresses the activity of seeing. And this active manner of seeing in turn expresses the viewer's presence inside the pictorialized space itself. What is represented, then, is not the church interior as such but the procedure of

its being perceived by the actively seeing subject who feels placed inside the depicted space. In this respect, Delaunay's series of Saint-Séverin pictures is an important solution to a Futurist problem formulated in 1910 in the Technical Manifesto of Futurist painting: "The artist has always shown objects and persons that were placed in front of us. We place the viewer right inside the picture."[32]

Every kind of perspective is an optical system which represents the world as seen. Looking at the church renderings of the seventeenth century, we find that they lack this sense of the viewer's being inside the depicted area which Delaunay's spatial representations convey. For in the lofty and significant view of a Gothic church interior, the rule of central perspective that all vertical lines must be painted as vertical necessarily produces a distance between the seeing and the seen. And actually, the world depicted by means of central perspective is not an exclusively subjective world; it is rather a kind of static reality that is seen by the subject but objectively arranged. In viewing one of Delaunay's pictures, however, the seeing subject experiences the pictorially represented world to the degree to which he is capable of sharing the experience of seeing with a moving eye, thanks to the deformation of the vertical lines.

Robert Delaunay himself, in explaining one of his Saint-Séverin pictures, spoke of a search for movement,[33] and Gleizes mentioned a plurality of perspective viewpoints which introduce a heretofore unknown factor, the factor of time *(le facteur temps)*, into painting.[34] Whether the element of time in pictorial representations of space is basically new or not, what Gleizes obviously meant is the passage of time connected with the subject's experience of being in motion while seeing, an experience made visible by the diminishing degree of curvature in successive rows of columns. But much as these graduated curvatures of the columns express pictorially the experience of being in motion while seeing, they also, it must be added, decorate the picture area in an immediately perceptible over-all way that is clear by being parabolically ornamental. Perhaps the best example of this is *Saint-Séverin No. 7* (plate 2).

But let us get to the decisive point: the viewer encounters in the picture his own motion-filled sight processes; these processes have been pictorially composed and are thus instantly evident. One might say the picture produces a formal objectification of utterly subjective experiences, and that this objectification becomes evident at a single glance, simultaneously. The viewer sees his own successive acts of seeing simultaneously in this picture.

The idea of simultaneity is a general idea of the period before World War I. In 1912, Arthur Barzun, probably influenced by Delaunay, attempted to define a type of literary drama combining "voice, song, and simultaneous rhythm."[35] In this particular kind of simultaneity, voices were to speak at the same time, harmoniously or with discordant effect. Later, in 1918, the Berlin Dadaist Manifesto stated, "The simultaneous poem teaches us the meaning of things in wildly crisscrossing activity; while Mr. Schulze reads, the Balkan Express crosses the bridge at Niš, a pig whimpers in the butcher Nuttke's cellar."[36] Delaunay himself said, with special reference to the poems of Apollinaire and Cendrars, that "Literary simultaneity can be produced by the use of word contrasts."[37]

Simultaneity was analytic Cubism's word for several views of the same object seen at the same time: for example, one section of a fruit bowl is seen from below, another in profile, and still another from the opposite side. Simultaneity of various actions turns up during that period in "chronophotographs" – popular at the time – that unfold a simple action. These might have given an impetus, among others, to Marcel Duchamp's above-mentioned *Nude Descending a Staircase*.[38] The idea of simultaneity applies to the artistic aims of Futurism, especially to its proclamation of a dynamic "complementarism" between object and environment which was to be created as a single entity by the picture.[39] Simultaneity is also the dominant theme in Delaunay's Eiffel Tower pictures. "So many viewpoints . . ." – Cendrars' brilliant description comes to mind.[40] One might even be tempted to discover simultaneity, in this last sense, in certain polyperspective systems of the seventeenth century in which several often incompatible prospects are combined. Jacob van Ruisdael's famous *Mill at Wijk near Duurstede*, the most famous mill in the history of art, would be a marvelous example of this: the landscape is seen panoramically, as from a great distance, while the mill itself is seen at close range from below, which emphasizes its towering monumentality. Where then does the idea of simultaneity really begin?

There are indubitably great differences between Futurism and Cubism under the common heading of simultaneity; there are even great differences between Delaunay's Saint-Séverin pictures and his Eiffel Towers. In the former, the various lines of vision in the picture have a certain direct continuity, thanks to the curves which diminish toward the background; the latter series contains an agglomeration, that is, a rather accidental piling up, of vantage points. But while we may interpret these paintings by Delaunay as polyperspective systems, and while they try to unify motion-filled or at least motion-given lines of vision into a single aspect, the artist himself, when he looked back at these works from a later artistic position, considered them all inwardly disrupted and in the final analysis catastrophic views.[41]

This remark dates from the year 1939, and the expression "catastrophic views" is linked to a specific reference to World War I. But this of course is merely a literary turn of phrase and does not mean that Delaunay ascribed any sort of prophetic dimension to the pictures. His judgment that they – and many Cubist and Futurist works as well – were failures is based on considerations of form only. His severely negative judgment was rooted in the idea that motion cannot be created by means of drawn objects. Motion, said Delaunay, must be achieved by meaningfully selected and meaningfully combined color values. He was also of the opinion – which may strike us as strange at first hearing – that not even film (motion-picture film) truly expresses motion.[42] But the very strangeness of this definition can clarify Delaunay's artistic aims for us: his striving for an optical expansion of perception and the creation of an altogether optical and exclusively inner-optical, unequivocal reality, for a "harmony of colors that separate and, in the same action, reunite into a whole." These are the words Paul Klee used in translating Delaunay's essay on "Light" of 1912, the artist's earliest and certainly his fundamental statement on the theory of art.[43]

When we now continue reading Delaunay's theoretical writings and find the statement that the true innovation in living, abstract art does not consist in drawing certain geometric figures, but only in the rhythm of color elements in a picture; and when we read that neither circles nor squares but only the visionary powers of color shapes arranged according to organic and rhythmic laws constitute a living work of abstract art,[44] then we understand another important fact: Delaunay did not unconditionally advocate nonobjective painting as such. His intentions were by no means directed toward a nonobjective, constructivist linearism. Delaunay did not consider abstract painting to be a quasimusical system; he did not regard colors as the equivalents of sounds, as did the German Romantics and Kandinsky after them. Neither did Delaunay strive for any sort of enlargement of psychical expression by means of nonobjective painting. He was not after emotion but rather after an intensification and expansion of sight. His aim was specific optic information such as can be found only in color sight. It has been said here earlier that Delaunay believed in a synchronic action[45] to be

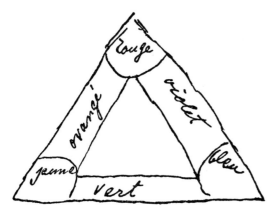

and yellow-violet. The eye produces its own complementary contrasts: if you look at a red color area on a white background for a little while and then cover it up with white, your eye will produce a green afterimage, complementary to the red. The eye adds green to red of its own accord. In the same way, it will produce orange to complement blue, and violet to complement yellow.

According to Goethe, the complementary contrasts are color totalities; each of those totalities contains one primary color in a pure state, and the other two in a mixed state. The eye encounters the sum of its own activity actualized in complementary contrasts.[53] The critic Théodore Silvestre was especially appreciative of Delacroix' use of complementary contrasts: "If green predominates in a figure on the shadow side, then red will predominate on the light side; if the light section of a figure is yellow, then the dark section is violet; if it is blue, then the opposite side will be orange."[54] Silvestre reported that Delacroix even used a color clock. And we feel we are getting very close to Delaunay's artistic program when we learn that Charles Blanc, in an essay on Delacroix, stressed that painters must be conversant with "the phenomena of simultaneous perception of colors."[55]

But we know that Delaunay's orientation toward color was largely based on the famous, frequently mentioned yet little-known color theory of Michel-Eugène Chevreul. This theory had interested Delacroix too. Later, through the work of Ogden N. Rood, it became of fundamental importance for Pointillism. Chevreul differentiated between "coloris vrai" (true coloring) and "coloris absolu" (absolute coloring) in painting. He explained that a painting can have an extremely agreeable effect owing to perfect color composition – that is, a color composition which corresponds with our sight – even when the colors used in the picture differ radically from the actual colors of the depicted objects.[56]

Chevreul's work on color theory discusses so-called simultaneous contrasts in the following way. If we look simultaneously at two zones of identical hue but varying degree of darkness, or at two zones of varying hue and identical degrees of darkness that are so close together their edges touch, then if these zones are not too large, the eye will perceive changes in color intensity in the first case and changes in hue in the second. The decisive factor is that different color zones, placed close together and seen simultaneously, will change their valences within the eye: "Now, as these modifications make the simultaneously perceived zones look much more different than they really are, I call them simultaneous contrast of colors."[57] Simultaneous contrast occurs – to give the simplest example first – when a light object appears lighter next to a dark object, and a dark object seems darker next to a light object, than each does when seen by itself. The same observation can be found in Goethe's color theory, thus: "A gray object on a black ground appears much lighter than on white. . . . When something dark is presented to the eye, the eye demands light; it demands dark when light is presented; and in this way it demonstrates its vitality, its right to grasp the object by producing something out of itself that contrasts with the object."[58]

Chevreul declared that a color is intensified when white is placed beside it, because the white light which makes the color paler is withdrawn from it, and that black placed next to a color reduces its intensity and can even syphon off its color altogether, as is the case with certain yellows.[59] A clear blue drives an adjoining yellow toward orange, while darker values of blue will weaken the same yellow and turn it green – "a perfectly simple effect when we consider that yellow becomes greener the paler it turns."[60] But Chevreul emphatically reminded the reader not to forget that these actions are neither "chemical" nor "physical" but always the result of a process that takes place in ourselves when we have a simultaneous perception of color values.[61]

Chevreul said further that colors and tones, when seen simultaneously, can achieve harmony of similarity and harmony of contrast. *Tone* signifies the various modifications which a color can undergo from its greatest intensity toward black or white. All the tones together form the *scale*, while the term *nuance* is applied to those modifications which a color undergoes when small amounts of another color are added to it.[62]

Harmony of similarity occurs when two related colors, such as red and red-orange, of identical tone level appear side by side, or when two related tone levels of one and the same red value appear side by side. Harmony of contrast occurs when two colors, related or even identical in quality but of the most different tone level, appear side by side.[63] But far more impressive is the effect when two complementary colors are placed side by side, especially when their tone levels are identical, which increases the contrast effect: "The complementary color arrangement is superior to all others in contrast harmony, and in order to produce the finest effect, the tones should be as similar in level as possible."[64] The color totality contained in complementary colors is the summit of all contrast harmony, for complementary colors reciprocally increase each other's intensity because each is the afterimage of the other.

Disharmony, on the other hand, occurs when two colors which are neither similar nor in complementary contrast with each other are seen side by side, such as red and yellow. To see such colors simultaneously is irritating to the eye: "Green, the complement of red, appears to be added to the yellow, which taken on a greenish tinge; blue-violet, the complement of yellow, appears added to the red and shifts the red toward violet."[65] A similar example is given in the prospectus of Chevreul's book: "If a sheet of blue paper is placed next to a yellow one, these two sheets by no means take on a green tinge, as we might suppose since we know that green is composed of a mixture of blue and yellow. Instead, the colors seem to tend toward red, so that the blue takes on a violet tint and the yellow an orange."[66]

This statement and many others, according to Chevreul, were not random accumulations of hypotheses of greater or less ingenuity, but the result of an *a posteriori* method: "The facts were observed, defined, and described, after which they began to generalize into a simple system which has all the qualities of a natural law."[67] This system is Chevreul's twelve-step color circle, on which each color is divided into twenty tone levels between black and white (see below). It all brings to mind Josef Albers' very topical paper on "The Interaction of Color."[68]

For Robert Delaunay, colors are the painter's actual language: "Color is form and subject."[69] In addition, Delaunay considered the language of color the most human language imaginable in art. Every human being, he said, is capable of being affected by the universal language of colors, by their play, movement, chords, rhythms – in short, by those arrangements that are especially suited to man's natural inclinations.[70] But getting back to the essential idea of synchronic action, we read: "The movements I mean – I experience them vividly; *I do not describe them*. Through their contrasts, they are simultaneous – not successive."[71] Delaunay

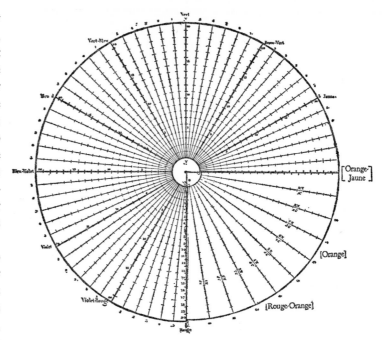

repeatedly spoke of the innate disposition of colors toward a "rhythmic simultaneity" which is differentiated within itself through different speed impulses: slow impulses for "complements" and quick ones for "dissonances."[72] Colors, he said, cause the sensual experience of a "synchronic movement which is the representation of the universal Drama."[73] In his essay "Painting Is the Original Language of Light," Delaunay spoke of a "perpetual movement" resulting from simultaneous contrasts.[74] And the expression *rhythmic simultaneity* occurs in his essay "Light."[75] He went on to say that a picture, as a simultaneously perceptible object, can contain a variety of dimensions owing to various color groups which oppose or neutralize each other, and that the intensity of vibration of each individual color depends on its relation to the color next to it and to all the other colors in the picture.[76] A remark of Guillaume Apollinaire's points toward a connection between simultaneity and light as a phenomenon of life: he said that simultaneity is life itself, and that every successive arrangement of elements is bound to lead toward the end, that is, toward death.[77]

Without doubt, the optical information related here is fairly complex. There remains, however, the general question of how necessary the knowledge of such a theory of painting, which leads from complexity to ever greater complexities, is for the viewer of an artist's painting, to guide him toward either more adequate sight or more adequate thoughts about what he sees. In his essay "Light," Delaunay himself admitted that what is needed is the will to see: "Let us try to see."[78]

6

Let us take as an example the picture *Circular Forms. Sun No. 1* (plate 12). This picture is a system of circular forms of which the most intensely colored form is shown whole, while three others, in paler colors, touch the complete form tangentially and at the same time, by being cut off at the picture margins, seem to reach beyond the viewer's field of vision. Both the gradation of color intensity and the potential extension of these circles beyond our field of vision express radiation from a center of energy. This is emphasized by a system of horizontal, vertical, and diagonal lines which structure the field of vision and connect the complete circle with its satellites. It is important for this integration that the interior order of the dominant circle detracts from its center: none of the lines point to that center. But just as the black arc, which is placed on the right of the central yellow and opened to the right, indicates the outlines of the satellite circles on the right, so the purple arc on the left of the central yellow seems to send similar impulses to the unpainted spaces on the left. Besides, both arcs appear as elements of a propeller shape in their special relation to the central yellow, and together with further impulses and counterimpulses playing around that central yellow, they express a rotating motion.

The intended color effects of the picture concern sensations of light, of simultaneity, of harmony, and at the same time of unevenness ("Light. Simultaneity. Harmony. Uneven"),[79] or – summed up – an organic form of color receptivity which forces the eye to open wide, so to say, and which can be experienced as simultaneous because it does not make us conscious of the successiveness of sight. To see this picture, we need not move our eyes in order to grasp the meaning of its parts as a whole, as we must in reading. Delaunay's picture lights up in the eye by its coloring; that is, the ubiquity of the whole is optically experienced as the glance takes in the colors individually and in their entirety. The colors, which are present in varying intensity, participate in disharmonic and harmonic contrasts. The latter are found in the cut-off circles where light yellow and red tones adjoin, for instance at the upper right, and also in the lower right-hand corner where light red and violet tones are placed side by side. But the green arc at bottom center stands rather in disharmony to its neighboring light violet tones, while it complements (that is, harmonizes with) the adjoining reddish arc. And while the blue near the lower left corner forms a heightened color polarity with that red arc, it also points to the more distant orange areas which complement it.

All the colors in the satellite circles are cooler reflections of the colors in the main circle: there, the adjoining red and blue form the greatest, most tension-filled color polarity in the picture. But this extreme challenge to the eye through color values is relaxed in turn by the added yellow, which is essential to the context of the picture, and which then produces the harmonic totality of the so-called three basic colors. These basic colors in turn correspond with their various complements; they direct the gaze toward them wherever they occurs near or far. The painter has manipulated optical provocations not for the sake of aesthetic playfulness but in order to express a "multiple rhythm"[80] which permeates nature itself, a multiple rhythm of that synchronic movement or synchronic action which has been mentioned here before. This means that the eye can see simultaneously how red complements and harmonizes with an adjoining green while reacting disharmonically and noncomplementarily to a neighboring blue, to the intensified excitement of the eye. This blue at the same time complements and harmonizes with an orange elsewhere in the picture. Hence this color group contains tensing and relaxing sensations which in turn and simultaneously are disturbed and pacified by further colors. And so the process repeats itself while yet – always simultaneously – all colors in all their multiple positive and negative constellations remain subordinated to a black which in our picture forms the absolute center of the composition and stands in the most radical polarity to an adjoining, almost colorless white value. The eye sees *simul et singulariter*.

This is also the case in the picture *Circular Forms. Sun and Moon* (plate 11), where sun and moon comprise the overarching polarity of the total composition as realms of heat and cold, as regions of activity and passivity, of action and rest. The lunar region, though only a section of it is shown, appears closed, receiving, not giving; and the sun is experienced in the everywhere recurrent, simultaneous, manifold, consonant and dissonant interplay of color energies. The sun is present as a continuous process, as concentrated activity; light intensity is not created by the number of light-colored values but by the quantity of contrast energies in what we see and, therefore, by the activation of our sight.

To the degree to which the eye sees colors not successively but simultaneously and experiences them singly and together in all the possibilities of their interplay in harmonies and disharmonies, in faster and slower impulses, to the same degree will the eye experience, according to Delaunay, that "vital movement of the world"[81] which presents and reveals itself not in succession but simultaneously. Only the color-sensitive eye is capable of such complex perception. This is why Delaunay remarked that aural perception is necessarily successive, mechanical as the ticking of a clock, and thus not sufficient for our knowledge of the universe.[82] But the eye can sensually experience the imagined vitality of the world as a simultaneous action of separation and reunion. Painting supplies the material through which the eye can experience all this, because painting can arrange the spectrum colors in a way which appropriately provokes the eye. This was Robert Delaunay's true task as a painter, as he saw it; and it is through this claim that we must understand Delaunay's pictures from 1912 to 1914.

Seen as philosophy, this artistic intention of Delaunay's leads very close to Henri Bergson, especially as Delaunay and Bergson both used the ideas of "simultaneity," "succession," and "duration." Delaunay's essay on light speaks of duration *(durée);* his explanation of why aural perception is insufficient for our knowledge of the universe is that hearing has no depth, and also – as he added in a footnote – no duration. Bergson himself defined duration as something internal, as the "indivisible and thus substantial continuity of the inner life current," as the unconditional opposite to every merely additive sequence of autonomous elements.[82]

It cannot be doubted that for Bergson, as for Delaunay, the actual symptom of duration is mediation, the intimate correspondence of the various elements with each other; that indeed, "duration" and "vital movement of the world" are one and the same. But their opinions differ in respect to the experience potential of duration. For Bergson, duration is a spiritual reality to be reached via "succession": it is a unit of experience. It is neither physiological nor rational in origin, but is rooted solely in consciousness. It refers to a progression in time, to a process of development that cannot be measured and is therefore irreversible. For reversibility presupposes simultaneity as a mechanical system that is indifferent to duration and independent of consciousness. Delaunay saw duration as sensual reality achieved through "simultaneity": for him, duration is purely physiological – it can be experienced within the eye alone. It is the permanently simultaneous appearance of all correspondences between the most various phenomena as they create a lasting total sensation that continually remains the same. On the same level of sensual perception, Delaunay regarded succession as a mere mechanical sequence.

And yet, from the viewpoint of physiological sight, Delaunay's paintings are the perfect visual illustration of Bergson's ideas. They bear witness to the radical

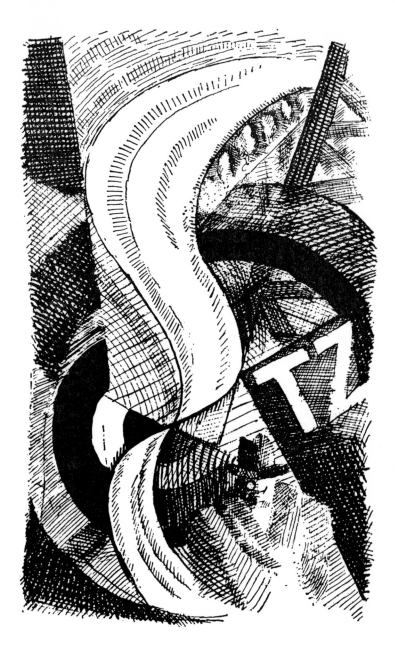

Propeller Form   1923

thesis that duration or vital movement of the world can be sensually experienced as visual reality which can be programmed by painting, and that in the realm of such purely sensual experience, duration can only be seen and not heard. This was Delaunay's belief. More than any other artist of his time, Robert Delaunay regarded the special optical information available through painting simply as incomparable information about the universe.

The aim of Chevreul's color guide was to achieve harmonies and avoid disharmony. What Chevreul still regarded as a guide to painting Delaunay, having enlarged the idea of harmony so that it included color conflict as an expressive value which must be part of the whole, saw in its totality. His wider color concept is historically relevant. We might say that, in the realm of active color vision as defined by Delaunay, the spectrum has a meaning similar to that of central perspective; it enlarges the presentation of reality in the dimension of color, just as central perspective enlarges it in linearism. The convergent lines of central perspective enormously aid representation because they show the finite as part of a potential infinite, by systematizing objects scattered through space and bringing them into relation to each other; just so do the colors of the spectrum, as they play to and away from each other, now clashing and now harmonizing, catch and synchronize various actions in a kind of steady and unceasing simultaneity of systole and diastole. Goethe said that he who "has discovered the principles of color has developed color harmony out of the systole and diastole for which the retina is formed, or in Plato's words, 'out of syncrisis and diacrisis.'"[84] In considering abstract painting as such, we might well ask ourselves whether the colorism which Delaunay strove for, applied practically and explained theoretically, might not express temporal simultaneity in the same way in which central perspective linearism expresses spatial homogeneity.[85]

7

The preceding reflections on the historic position of Robert Delaunay's art were based on a model of various color systems in art and on various levels of demand made on the eye by painting: there is a first level, at which colors are easily accessible to the eye's habit; but a second level challenges the eye to the very limit of its capacity. At this level, sight becomes a conscious activity which in turn activates what we see. Delaunay's position is characteristic of that second level, especially in his Orphic period, when he created his circular forms, and also in his window pictures. The intention in each case is that the picture always look "new," that it not be regarded as existing once and for all but as creating itself over and over again – a permanent renewal of identity. This is how we may perhaps understand what Delaunay himself called "form in motion, static – and dynamic."[86] And while at that first level of visual challenge light is represented in a rather pictorial way, the second level uses color to cause a kind of vitality within the eye which corresponds with the energy of light. This too has been discussed before. It might be added that the window pictures, in which light is refracted into colors, show a definite though certainly unintention-

al family resemblance to those typically French light allegories in which the world is seen in a mirror or through some other kind of reflection – in other words, is not shown through direct mimetic media.[87]

The newest history of art allows us to speak of yet a third level, at which the eye is challenged to the point of noticeable overstrain and which actually creates a sensation of pain. This third level of challenge to the eye occasionally becomes the picture theme in so-called Op art, as in certain works by Victor Vasarely.[88] Here we no longer experience a continual renewal of identity or – as far as the suggestion of light is concerned – an uninterrupted intensity of brilliance, but rather a repeated, jumping change of appearances, an optic irritation as if the eye were blinded by too much light. According to Vasarely, this kind of optic irritation fulfills the theoretically formulated demand that painting must take part, no matter to what modest degree, in the "multidimensional plastic" where form and nonform, vagueness and clarity, "l'informel et le formel" keep alternating to the point of incomprehensibility.[89] "Multiple rhythm" – that was Delaunay's formulation in a different though not so very remote historical situation.

In the system of the three possible levels of challenge to the eye, Delaunay's pictures of 1912 to 1914 occupy a place between the traditional and the modern. Delaunay never aimed at optic irritation. For if optic irritation might be regarded as continuous ambiguity allowing of no single meaning since the very forms seem to keep losing the conditions of their own existence,[90] Delaunay's pictures might be said to consolidate a multiplicity of meanings into a single meaning – a single meaning that contains within itself a multiplicity of meanings.

Within the framework of an almost overgreat challenge to the eye, Delaunay tried, in the years after 1914, to develop objective paintings out of his circular forms, using both human figures and still lifes in order to reconcretize the objective world from basically nonobjective color shapes (plate 15). This attempt at reobjectification goes beyond object combinations as they occur in his *Cardiff Team* pictures, for instance; it was an attempt to "raise the circular forms to the rank of a universal formula."[91] While Delaunay himself saw in his 1914 *Homage to Blériot* a "wealth of intense life," a "poetry that cannot be expressed in words," even a "motor, a departure," and "power of sun and power of earth," he described his figure pictures of 1915 as "utilizing" these pictorial "discoveries in the depiction of man." Man, he explained, is "not copied, nor drawn, nor detached from his surroundings," and this is so because of the "flowing spatial relationships" of everything in the picture. He said further that these objects draw "their vitality from color"; they are "not forms taken from a dictionary or a manufacturer's catalog."[92] Historically speaking, one might see a connection between this reobjectification and the so-called deductive method of Juan Gris, in the very general sense that Gris too strove to gain objective forms from nonobjective form combinations: "Until now, pictures have always been made from objects, but my working method is the exact opposite. . . . The mathematics of pictorial methods lead me toward the representation of objects. . . . Only in being my own viewer can I extract the object from my picture."[93] But Gris' pictures lack those basic round or rounded spectrum color shapes that positively invite cosmic associations and are typical of Delaunay's pictures.

Whether these special color shapes facilitate a reobjectification of the picture world, or whether they make it more difficult or even impossible, the fact remains that Delaunay soon turned his back on these attempts. In the 1930s, in his *Rhythm without End* and *Joy of Life* series, he discovered utterly nonobjective, perfectly simple, clear, anonymously geometric, and homogeneously colored figurations.

The picture *Rhythm. "Joy of Life"* (plate 16) is obviously related to *Circular Forms. Sun No. 1* (plate 12). The composition is a large structure consisting of rounded color bands which have attracted four smaller discs through what we might call a kind of magnetism. The picture center contains yet another smaller disc which seems to be in the process of forming and which figures as the origin of the large structure. The small discs at the upper and lower right have partial halos – that is, they are accompanied part way by color paths which themselves swing into the main structure of the picture. In addition to these circular pictorial values, Delaunay's composition also has horizontal, vertical, and diagonal values which interfere with the rotations in order to produce an expression of heightened energy. The vertical line through the center is the only line that runs all the way through the picture; it cuts the picture into two halves which are partly in alignment and partly shifted out of alignment. Even in its linear structure, Delaunay's composition shows an interaction of harmonies and disharmonies: what obstructs in one direction continues in another; what disrupts one form complements another. The coloring enlivens our vision, and our vitalized eye in turn enlivens what it sees. But all color values appear dominated by a black area which lies slightly off-center and which, paired with a white area in the very center of the picture, constitutes the picture's greatest polarity: if we try to replace this black with any other color, let us say blue or green, the entire picture loses both contrast and luminosity.

The picture *Rhythm without End* (fig. 30) confirms what Delaunay wrote in a letter of 1941 about his later works:

They are chords, created out of the contrasting and dissonant reciprocities of circular forms, in the purest and strictest meaning of the word. . . . The colors are arranged according to intensity, number, and measure. The harmonization of these measures gives the rhythm – this is where time is introduced into the picture structure. . . . This art combines perfectly with architecture, indeed it *is* architecture, for it is based on architectonic color laws.[94]

No less than the compositions by Auguste Herbin, Delaunay's late style anticipates in color and form that pictorial language which we appreciate today in works by Morris Louis, Robert Indiana, Frank Stella, Kenneth Noland, or Ellsworth Kelly.

1   W. Schöne, *Über das Licht in der Malerei*, 2nd ed., Berlin, 1961, p. 219.

2   H. Sedlmayr, "Zeichen der Sonne," *Epochen und Werke*, Vienna, 1960, II, 255.

3   H. Sedlmayr, "Das Licht in seinen künstlerischen Manifestationen," *Studium Generale*, XIII, 1960, p. 323.

4   Max Imdahl, "Die Rolle der Farbe in der neueren französischen Malerei: Abstraktion und Konkretion," in *Immanente Ästhetik – Ästhetische Reflexion*, vol. 2 of *Poetik und Hermeneutik*, Munich, 1966, pp. 195 ff.; Faber Birren, *History of Color in Painting, with New Principles of Color Expression*, New York, 1965.

5   Robert Delaunay, *Du Cubisme à l'art abstrait*, ed. by Pierre Francastel, Paris, 1957, p. 146. In a letter to Franz Marc of January 11, 1913, Delaunay said that the Impressionists tried to re-create light – "recréer la lumière" (*ibid.*, p. 188).

6   *Ibid.*, pp. 146 (see above, p. 9), 180, 115.

7   Victor Vasarely, "Formel–Informel," 1956; in M. Joray, *Vasarely*, Neuchâtel, 1965, p. 61.

8   José Ortega y Gasset, "Der Gesichtspunkt und seine Rolle in der Kunst," *Merkur*, 1947, p. 519.

9   Cited in Gaston Diehl, *Matisse*, Munich, 1958, p. 94.

10 Jules Laforgue, "Critique d'art: L'Impressionnisme," *Mélanges posthumes*, Paris, 1913, pp. 133–34.

11 Quoted in Walter Hess, *Paul Cézanne: Über die Kunst, Gespräche mit Gasquet und Briefe*, Hamburg, 1957, pp. 113, 80.

12 Arnold Gehlen, *Zeit-Bilder*, 2nd ed., Frankfurt am Main, 1965, p. 62.

13 H. Sedlmayr, *Verlust der Mitte*, Salzburg, 1948, p. 125.

14 John Ruskin, *The Elements of Drawing*, London, 1856; see E. H. Gombrich, *Art and Illusion*, Washington, D.C., 1960, p. 296.

15 Kurt Badt, *Die Kunst Cézannes*, Munich, 1954, p. 132.

16 Letter dated October 9, 1907; see H. Meyer, "Rilkes Cézanne-Erlebnis," in *Jahrbuch für Ästhetik und allgem. Kunstwissenschaft*, II, 1954, 165.

17 Quoted in E. Bernard, *Souvenirs sur Cézanne*, Paris, 1926, p. 61.

18 J. A. D. Ingres, *Pensées et écrits du peintre*, Geneva, 1947, p. 60.

19 Karl von Pidoll, *Aus der Werkstatt eines Künstlers: Erinnerungen an den Maler Hans von Marées . . .* , Augsburg, 1930, p. 78.

20 Konrad Fiedler, *Schriften zur Kunst*, ed. by H. Marbach, Leipzig, 1896, pp. 55, 248, 44.

21 Adolf von Hildebrand, *Das Problem der Form in der bildenden Kunst*, Strasbourg, 1893, p. 22.

22 See *Dokumentationen über Marcel Duchamp*, catalog of the exhibition at the Kunstgewerbemuseum, Zurich, 1960, p. 27.

23 Albert Gleizes, *Kubismus* (Bauhausbücher 13), Munich, 1928, text below fig. 5.

24 See Delaunay, *op. cit.*, p. 228.

25 F. W. Heckmanns, *Pieter Janszoon Saenredam: Das Problem seiner Raumform*, Recklinghausen, 1965.

26 See above, p. 26.

27 Pierre Francastel, in Delaunay, *op. cit.*, p. 22.

28 *Ibid.*, pp. 72, 87.

29 Umberto Boccioni, quoted in Ch. Baumgarth, *Geschichte des Futurismus*, Hamburg, 1966, pp. 210–11.

30 Erwin von Busse, *Der Blaue Reiter*, documentary new ed. by K. Lankheit, Munich, 1965, pp. 97–98.

31 Georg Schmidt, *Robert Delaunay*, Baden-Baden, 1964, p. 8. Paul Bommersheim, "Die Überwindung der Perspektive und Robert Delaunay," *Der Sturm*, III, no. 148–49, February, 1913, repeatedly stressed the importance of a "vital manner of viewing."

32 Quoted in Baumgarth, *op. cit.*, p. 182.

33 Delaunay, *op. cit.*, p. 228.

34 See *ibid.*

35 See *ibid.*, p. 112.

36 Quoted in H. Richter, *Dada: Kunst und Antikunst*, Cologne, 1964, p. 109.

37 Delaunay, *op. cit.*, p. 112.

38 R. Lebel, *Marcel Duchamp*, Cologne, 1962, p. 16.

39 See Baumgarth, *op. cit.*, pp. 183, 210, 213.

40 See above, p. 29.

41 Delaunay, *op. cit.*, p. 229.

42 *Ibid.*, p. 229; see also p. 189.

43 Robert Delaunay, "Über das Licht," free tr. into German by Paul Klee of "La Lumière," *Der Sturm*, III, no. 144–45, January, 1913.

44 Delaunay, *Du Cubisme à l'art abstrait*, p. 95.

45 *Ibid.*, p. 140.

46 *Ibid.*, p. 75.

47 Giovanni Pietro Bellori, *Le Vite de' Pittori, Scultori ed Architetti moderni*, 1672; Rome, 1728, p. 14.

48 A. Fontaine, *Conférences inédites de l'Académie Royale de Peinture et de Sculpture*, Paris, 1903, pp. 35 ff.

49 Roger de Piles, *Sur le Coloris*, Paris, 1673; quoted in *Recueil de divers ouvrages sur la peinture et le coloris*, Paris, 1775, p. 194.

50 Charles Baudelaire, "Exposition universelle de 1855," in *Oeuvres complètes*, Éd. Crepet, Paris, 1925, VI, 248–49.

51 Delaunay, *Du Cubisme à l'art abstrait*, p. 158.

52 Charles Blanc, *Les Artistes de mon temps*, Paris, 1867, p. 50.

53 J. W. von Goethe, "Didaktischer Teil," *Farbenlehre*, 808.

54 Quoted in Paul Signac, *D'Eugène Delacroix au Néo-impressionnisme*, 1899; Paris, 1911, p. 23.

55 Blanc, *op. cit.*, p. 62.

56 M. E. Chevreul, *De la Loi du contraste simultané des couleurs, et de l'assortiment des objets colorés, considéré d'après cette loi dans ses rapports avec la peinture, les tapisseries des Gobelins, les tapisseries de Beauvais pour meubles, les tapis, la mosaïque, les vitraux colorés, l'impression des étoffes, l'imprimerie, l'enluminure, la décoration des édifices, l'habillement et l'horticulture*, Paris, 1839, pp. 183–84; see also O. N. Rood, *Student's Text-Book of Color*, New York, 1879; and M. E. Chevreul, *The Principles of Harmony and Contrast of Colors, and Their Applications to the Arts*, ed. by Faber Birren, New York, 1967.

57 Chevreul, *De la Loi . . .* , p. 7.

58 Goethe, *op. cit.*, 38.

59 Chevreul, *De la Loi . . .* , p. 198.

60 *Ibid.*, p. 201.

61 *Ibid.*, p. 14.

62 *Ibid.*, p. 84.

63 *Ibid.*, p. 109.

64 *Ibid.*, p. 135.

65 *Ibid.*, pp. 20–21

66 *Ibid.*, prospectus, p. 2.

67 *Ibid.*, p. XI.

68 Josef Albers, "The Interaction of Color," New Haven and London, 1963.

69 Delaunay, *Du Cubisme à l'art abstrait*, p. 67.

70 *Ibid.*, pp. 218–19.

71 *Ibid.*, p. 184.

72 *Ibid.*, p. 184.

73 *Ibid.*, p. 180.

74 *Ibid.*, p. 168.

75 *Ibid.*, p. 146; see above, p. 9.

76 *Ibid.*, p. 60.

77 *Ibid.*, p. 157.

78 *Ibid.*, p. 146; see above, p. 9.

79 *Ibid.*, p. 143.

80 *Ibid.*, p. 140.

81 *Ibid.*, p. 146; see above, p. 9.

82 *Ibid.*

83 *Ibid.*, pp. 146, 147, 149; Henri Bergson, "La Pensée et le mouvant," *Oeuvres*, Paris, 1959, p. 1273; see also his "Essai sur les données immédiates de la conscience," *ibid.*, pp. 3 ff.

84 J. W. von Goethe, *Schriften zur Kunst*, memorial edition of the works, letters, and conversations, ed. E. Beutler, Zurich, 1954, XIII, 332–33.

85 See K. von Fischer, "Das Zeitproblem in der Musik," in *Das Zeitproblem im 20. Jahrhundert* (Dalp Collection, vol. 96), Bern, 1964, p. 310. Referring to the music of Arnold Schönberg in the early twenties, this author speaks of a "structure in the sense of a purely present structure, in which there is – at least at first – no longer any dynamically final course, but rather an unfolding of current and remembered things."

86 Delaunay, *Du Cubisme à l'art abstrait*, p. 75.

87 Sedlmayr, "Zeichen der Sonne," p. 254.

88 A typical example is the picture *Charga*, 1965, colorplate, in the catalog *Tendenzen struktaraler Kunst*, Westfälischer Kunstverein, Münster, 1966.

89 Joray, *loc. cit.*

90 H. van Lier, "Vasarely," *Quadrum*, XVII, n.d., 56; this contains many outstanding color illustrations.

91 I have taken this expression from Gustav Vriesen's notes.

92 Delaunay, *Du Cubisme à l'art abstrait*, pp. 63–64.

93 Quoted in Daniel-Henry Kahnweiler, *Der Weg zum Kubismus*, Stuttgart, 1958, p. 102.

94 Delaunay, *Du Cubisme à l'art abstrait*, p. 42.

Biographical Outline

Adapted from the catalog of the Robert Delaunay exhibition, Kunsthalle, Bern, July 27–September 2, 1951.

1885   Born April 12 in Paris. Both parents belong to the fashionable aristocratic society of Paris. After their divorce, Delaunay is raised by his mother's older sister while his mother travels extensively in India, Russia, and Africa.

1902   After very meager scholastic success in various secondary schools, he becomes an apprentice in a studio for decorative painting in Belleville.

1904   Vacation in Saint-Guénolé, Brittany. First landscape pictures.

1905   First self-portrait.

1905–7   Involvement with Neoimpressionism. Acquaintance with Jean Metzinger. *Young Girl; Night Scene*. Delaunay studies M. E. Chevreul's color theory. Meets Henri Rousseau; his mother, reporting on her travels in India, inspires Rousseau to paint *The Snake Charmer*. Delaunay meets his future wife, Sonia Uhde-Terk.

1907–8   Military training and service as a library assistant in Laon. First studies of the Cathedral of Laon.

1908   Under the influence of Paul Cézanne, Georges Seurat, and Henri Rousseau, Delaunay gradually abandons Fauvism. Flower still lifes.

1909–10   *The Spire of Notre-Dame, Saint-Séverin, City*, and *Eiffel Tower* series mark the beginning of his distinctively personal development. Delaunay calls this new phase his "transition period from Cézanne to Cubism" or his "destructive period."

1910   Marriage to Sonia Terk.

1911   Elisabeth Epstein, a friend of Alexej von Jawlensky's and Vasily Kandinsky's, introduces Delaunay to the Munich circle of the Blaue Reiter. On Kandinsky's invitation, Delaunay takes part in the first exhibition of the Blaue Reiter with the *Eiffel Tower* of 1910 (destroyed in 1945), *Saint-Séverin No. 1* of 1909, *The City No. 2* of 1909–10, and *The City* of 1911. From this moment on, Delaunay exerts a definite influence on August Macke, Franz Marc, and Paul Klee. Friendship with Guillaume Apollinaire, Henri Le Fauconnier, and Albert Gleizes.

1912   Delaunay spends a month in Laon. Series of pictures of the Cathedral of Laon. First one-man show. He paints the huge picture *The City of Paris* for the Salon des Indépendants, which concludes his "destructive period." The Window pictures inaugurate his "construction period." Arp, Macke, Marc, Klee, and the Berlin art patron Bernhard Köhler visit Delaunay in Paris. *Disc* of 1912.

1913   In January, Delaunay and Apollinaire travel to Berlin to the opening of the Delaunay exhibition in the gallery of *Der Sturm*. Apollinaire gives a lecture on modern art there. Delaunay's *The Cardiff Team* in the Salon des Indépendants. Circular-form pictures. The *Disc* and a simultaneous sculpture at the first German Herbstsalon in Berlin. Friendship with Blaise Cendrars.

1914   *Homage to Blériot*. Delaunay takes a trip to Spain (Fuenterrabia), where he is caught by the war.

1915–17   He lives alternately in Spain and Portugal. Series of *Nude Woman Reading, Portuguese Still Life, Portuguese Woman*, and *Barmaid*. Friendship with Sergei Diaghilev, Waslaw Nijinsky, Igor Stravinsky, Manuel de Falla, Diego Rivera.

1918   Décor for *Cléopâtre*, performed by the Ballet Russe. Costumes by Sonia Delaunay. Portrait of Stravinsky. Correspondence with the Dadaists Tristan Tzara, Philippe Soupault, and others.

1921   Return to Paris.

1922   Big exhibition at Paul Guillaume's gallery. Beginning of second series of Eiffel Tower pictures.

1923   Portraits of Claire and Ivan Goll, Bella Chagall, Tristan Tzara.

1924   End of second series of Eiffel Tower pictures. Beginning of the *Runner* series. Views of Paris from the roof of the Louvre. Acquaintance with Jules Supervielle and Joseph Delteil.

1925   Delaunay and Fernand Léger paint frescoes for the Palais de l'Ambassade de France at the Exposition Internationale d'Art Décoratif.

1926   Second *Runner* series.

1927   Series of portraits of Madame Jacques Heim.

1928   The American collector Solomon R. Guggenheim buys a *Tower* of 1910 for his museum of nonobjective paintings. Today there are more than thirty of Delaunay's pictures in that collection, but like some works by Arp, Klee, Braque, and Seurat that are not completely nonobjective, they are not exhibited.

1929   Delaunay stays in Carnac with Arp, Sophie Taeuber-Arp, and Tristan Tzara.

1930–35   Series of multicolored discs, among them *Joy of Life*. He begins his series of plaster reliefs and of Rhythm pictures. Panels of Dr. Paul Viard.

1935–37   Sketches and plans for wall decorations at the Paris World's Fair.

1937   With a team of fifty painters, Delaunay completes the decorations for the Palais des Chemins de Fer and the Palais de l'Air – a total of more than 27,000 square feet – in two months.

1938   With Gleizes, André Lhote, and Jacques Villon, Delaunay does the decorations for the sculpture hall of the Salon des Tuileries. The three panels in the form of a triptych are Delaunay's last works.

1939   Organizes with Nelly van Doesburg and others the first Salon des Réalités Nouvelles.

1940   Flees to the Auvergne and later to Mougins, near Cannes. Beginning of an unidentifiable illness.

1941   Dies on October 25, in a clinic in Montpellier.

The Countess Delaunay in her Paris apartment

Robert Delaunay aged eighteen

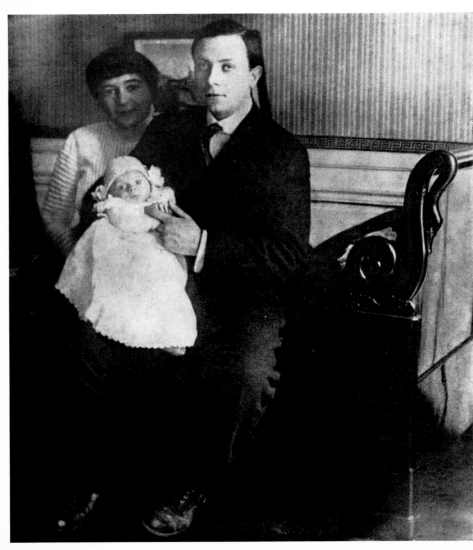

Sonia, Robert, and Charles Delaunay, February, 1911

The artist in 1925

The artist in 1924

Sonia Delaunay-Terk

Simultaneous automobile

1 Landscape of La Ronchère (Le Lavoir) 1904

2 Breton Woman 1904

3 Breton Woman. Seaweed Gatherer 1905

4 Portrait of Jean Metzinger *or* The Man with the Tulip   1906

5 Landscape with Disc   1906

6 Night Scene *or* The Horse-Drawn Carriage   1906—7

7 Landscape near Saint-Cloud 1910

8 Saint-Séverin No. 1 1909

9 Saint-Séverin No. 4 1909

10 Saint-Séverin No. 3 1909

11 Saint-Séverin No. 5 (The Rainbow) 1909—10

12   Eiffel Tower [with Trees]   1909

13 City (First Study) 1909

14 Study for "The City of Paris" 1909

15 The City No. 2 1909—10

16   The City   1911

17   Window on the City No. 4   1910–11

18   Street in Laon   1912

19   Street in Laon   1912

20   The Towers of Laon   1912

21 The Three Windows, the Tower, and the Ferris Wheel 1912

22 The Windows 1912

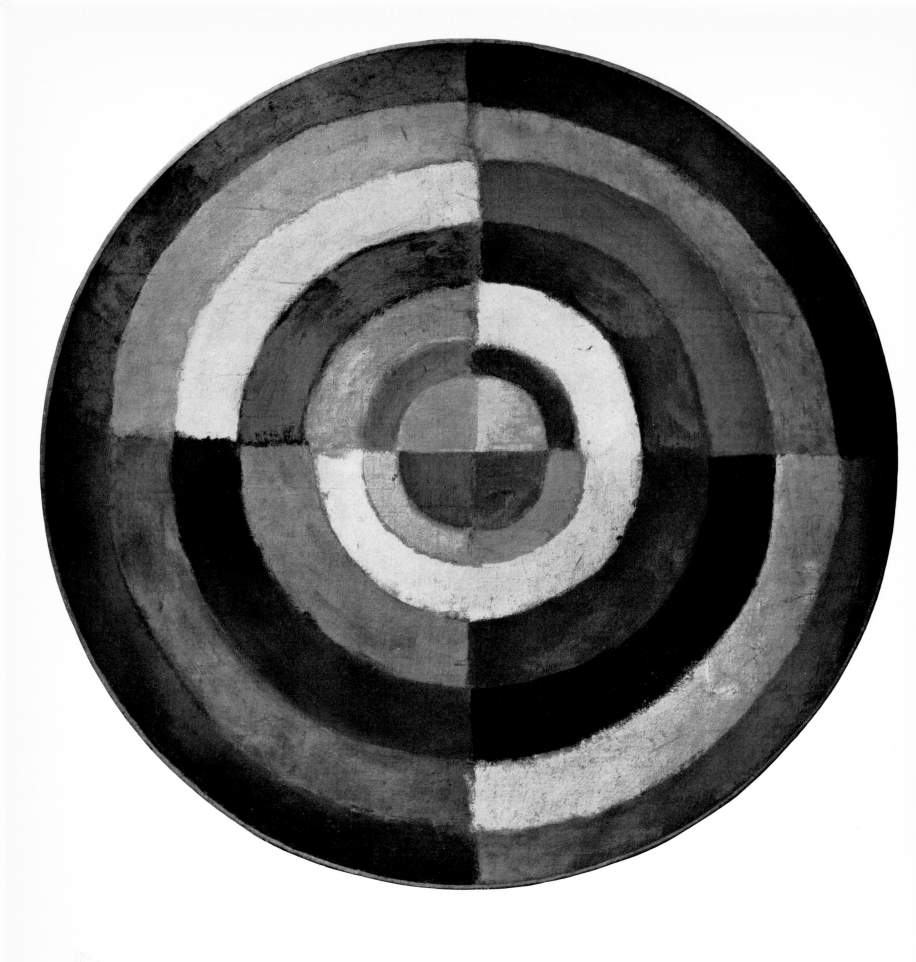

23 Disc 1912

24 Circular Forms (Sun) No. 3 1912

25 Circular Forms (Sun) 1913

26 Circular Forms (Moon) No. 2 1913

27 Circular Forms (Moon) No. 1 1913

28 Circular Forms 1930

29 Circular Forms 1912—30

30   Rhythm without End   1934

31 Rhythms 1934

32 Breton Woman (Study) 1904

33 The Sea (The Rocks) 1905

34 The Sea 1905

35 Breton Landscape
(The Church) 1905

36 Breton Landscape
(The Market) 1905

37 Self-Portrait with
Japanese Print 1905

38 Self-Portrait 1906

39 Self-Portrait 1908

40 Young Girl or The Poet
1906 or 1907

41 Portrait of Wilhelm Uhde 1907

42 Portrait of Madame Carlier
1905—6

43 Portrait of Monsieur
Henri Carlier 1906

44 Nudes with Ibises 1907

45 Still Life with Parrot 1907

46 Still Life with Gloves 1906—7

47 Still Life, Vases and Objects 1907

48 Landscape of Saint-Cloud 1910   49 The Dirigible and the Tower 1909   50 The Spire of Notre-Dame 1909   51 The Spire of Notre-Dame 1909—14

52 The Tower (First Study) 1909   53 Eiffel Tower 1910   54 The Three Graces 1909   55 The Three Graces (Study) 1912

56 Windows 1912

57 Windows on the City (First Part. First Simultaneous Contrasts) 1912

58 Windows on the City (First Part, Second Motif) 1912

59 Windows 1912

60 Circular Forms. Sun 1914

61 Circular Forms. Moon No. 3 1913

62 Rainbow 1913

63 Simultaneous Dress 1913—14

64 Simultaneous Dress 1914

65 Political Drama 1914

66 Football [Soccer] 1917—18

67 Third Version. The Cardiff Team 1913

68 Football [Soccer] 1917

69 Football [Soccer]. The Cardiff Team 1922—23

70 Carrousel with Pigs or Electric Carrousel 1922

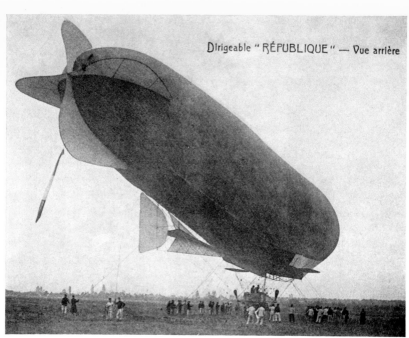

Eiffel Tower with airplane

Dirigible

The spire of Notre-Dame

Documents to Delaunay's Motifs

Soccer game

Political drama

List of Illustrations

The number in parentheses after the date refers to the catalog of Delaunay's work by Guy Habasque in Robert Delaunay, *Du Cubisme à l'Art abstrait*, ed. by Pierre Francastel, Paris, 1957.

Colorplates

Black-and-White Figures

23 *Disc – Disque.* 1912 (113)
Oil on canvas, diameter 52³/₄″. Collection Mr. and Mrs. Burton G. Tremaine, Meriden, Conn.

24 *Circular Forms (Sun) No. 3 – Formes circulaires (Soleil) no. 3.* 1912 (122)
Oil on canvas, 31⁷/₈ × 25⁵/₈″. Collection Professor W. Löffler, Zurich

25 *Circular Forms (Sun) – Formes circulaires (Soleil).* 1913 (128)
Watercolor on cardboard, 23¹/₄ × 18¹/₈″. Collection Bing, Paris

26 *Circular Forms (Moon) No. 2 – Formes circulaires (Lune) no. 2.* 1913 (131)
Oil on canvas, 31⁷/₈ × 25⁵/₈″. Collection Bing, Paris

27 *Circular Forms (Moon) No. 1 – Formes circulaires (Lune) no. 1.* 1913 (130)
Oil on canvas, 25⁵/₈ × 21¹/₄″. Collection Bing, Paris

28 *Circular Forms – Formes circulaires.* 1930 (271)
Oil on canvas, 97⁵/₈ × 181¹/₂″. Collection F. Meyer, Zurich

29 *Circular Forms – Formes circulaires.* 1912–30 (269)
Oil on canvas, 26⁵/₈ × 43¹/₄″. Collection Louis Carré, Paris

30 *Rhythm without End – Rythme sans fin.* 1934 (305)
Oil on canvas, 78³/₄ × 39³/₈″. Collection Sonia Delaunay, Paris

31 *Rhythms – Rythmes.* 1934 (326)
Oil on canvas, 63³/₄ × 51¹/₈″. Galerie Beyeler, Basel

32 *Breton Woman (Study) – Bretonne (Étude).* 1904 (4)
Pencil and oil on canvas, 21¹/₄ × 17″. Collection Sonia Delaunay, Paris

33 *The Sea (The Rocks) – La Mer (Les Rochers).* 1905 (18)
Oil on canvas, 14³/₄ × 21¹/₂″. Collection Sonia Delaunay, Paris

34 *The Sea – La Mer.* 1905 (17)
Oil on canvas, 25¹/₂ × 31⁷/₈″. Collection Sonia Delaunay, Paris

35 *Breton Landscape (The Church) – Paysage de Bretagne (L'Église).* 1905 (19)
Oil on canvas, 23¹/₄ × 24³/₄″. Collection Louis Carré, Paris

36 *Breton Landscape (The Market) – Paysage de Bretagne (Le Marché).* 1905 (20)
Oil on canvas, 14⁷/₈ × 18¹/₈″. Collection Sonia Delaunay, Paris

37 *Self-Portrait with Japanese Print – Autoportrait à l'estampe japonaise.* About 1905 (13)
Oil on canvas, 28³/₄ × 19¹/₈″. Collection Sonia Delaunay, Paris

38 *Self-Portrait – Autoportrait.* 1906 (29)
Oil on canvas, 21⁵/₈ × 18¹/₈″. Collection Sonia Delaunay, Paris

39 *Self-Portrait – Autoportrait.* 1908 (39)
Oil on canvas, 26 × 21⁷/₈″. Collection Sonia Delaunay, Paris

40 *Young Girl* or *The Poet – Fillette* or *La Poétesse.* 1906 or 1907 (33)
Oil on canvas, 28³/₄ × 19¹/₈″. Private collection, Paris

41 *Portrait of Wilhelm Uhde – Portrait de Wilhelm Uhde.* 1907 (34)
Oil on canvas, 31³/₈ × 25¹/₂″. Collection Sonia Delaunay, Paris

42 *Portrait of Madame Carlier – Portrait de Mme. Carlier.* 1905–6 (24)
Oil on canvas, 24³/₄ × 23¹/₄″. Collection Pierre Durelle, Paris

43 *Portrait of Monsieur Henri Carlier – Portrait de M. Henri Carlier.* 1906 (25)
Oil on canvas, 25¹/₄ × 23⁵/₈″. Musée National d'Art Moderne, Paris

44 *Nudes with Ibises – Nus aux ibis.* 1907 (35)
Oil on canvas, 21⁵/₈ × 18¹/₈″. Collection Louis Carré, Paris

45 *Still Life with Parrot – Nature morte au perroquet.* 1907 (36)
Oil on canvas, 31¹/₂ × 25⁵/₈″. Collection Louis Carré, Paris

46 *Still Life with Gloves – Nature morte aux gants.* 1906–7 (32)
Oil on canvas, 39³/₈ × 31⁷/₈″. Collection Louis Carré, Paris

47 *Still Life, Vases and Objects – Nature morte, Vases et objets.* 1907 (37)
Oil on canvas, 16⁷/₈ × 13″. Collection Sonia Delaunay, Paris

48 *Landscape of Saint-Cloud – Saint-Cloud (Étude).* 1910 (80)
Oil on cardboard, 22¹/₂ × 12³/₄″. Musée National d'Art Moderne, Paris. Delaunay Donation

49 *The Dirigible and the Tower – Dirigeable et la Tour.* 1909 (68)
Oil on cardboard, 13³/₄ × 10¹/₂″. Collection Sonia Delaunay, Paris

50 *The Spire of Notre-Dame – La Flèche de Notre-Dame.* 1909 (49)
Oil on canvas. Private collection, location unknown

51 *The Spire of Notre-Dame – La Flèche de Notre-Dame.* 1909–14 (145)
Wax on canvas, 22⁷/₈ × 15″. Collection Marguerite Arp-Hagenbach, Basel

52 *The Tower (First Study) – La Tour (Première étude).* 1909 (69)
Oil on canvas, 18¹/₈ × 15″. Collection Sonia Delaunay, Paris

53 *Eiffel Tower – Tour Eiffel.* 1910 (83)
Oil on canvas, 45¹/₄ × 31⁷/₈″. Private collection, Krefeld

54 *The Three Graces – Les trois Grâces.* 1909 (74)
Oil on canvas, 39³/₈ × 31⁷/₈″. Collection Bing, Paris

55 *The Three Graces (Study) – Les trois Grâces (Étude).* 1912 (98)
Oil on paper, mounted on canvas, 74 × 54¹/₂″. Collection Sonia Delaunay, Paris

56 *Windows – Les Fenêtres.* 1912 (351)
Gouache on paper, 16⁷/₈ × 32¹/₄″. Collection A. Chenu, Florence

57 *Windows on the City (First Part. First Simultaneous Contrasts) – Les Fenêtres sur la Ville (Première partie. Premiers contrastes simultanés).* 1912 (118)
Watercolor, 20¹/₂ × 81¹/₂″. Collection A. Chenu, Florence

58 *Windows on the City (First Part, Second Motif) – Les Fenêtres sur la Ville (1ᵉ partie, 2ᵉ motif).* 1912 (104)
Oil on cardboard, 15 × 11¹/₄″. Collection Sonia Delaunay, Paris

59 *Windows – Les Fenêtres.* 1912 (111)
Oil on canvas, oval 22¹/₂ × 48³/₈″. Collection Peggy Guggenheim, Venice

60 *Circular Forms. Sun – Formes circulaires. Soleil.* 1914 (746)
Wax on canvas, 9 × 7¹/₈″. Collection Lebel, Paris

61 *Circular Forms. Moon No. 3 – Formes circulaires. Lune no. 3.* 1913 (132)
Wax on canvas, 10 × 8¹/₄″. Collection Sonia Delaunay, Paris

62 *Rainbow – Arc-en-ciel.* 1913 (127)
Oil on canvas, 34⁵/₈ × 39³/₈″. Collection Bing, Paris

63 *Simultaneous Dress – Robe simultanée.* 1913–14 (362)
Lacquer on cardboard, 13 × 8⁵/₈″. Private collection, location unknown

64 *Simultaneous Dress – Robe simultanée.* 1914 (363)
Lacquer on paper, mounted on cardboard, 12 × 10³/₄″. Städtisches Kunsthaus, Bielefeld

65 *Political Drama – Drame politique.* 1914 (149)
Collage and oil on paper, 34⁷/₈ × 26³/₈″. Collection Mr. and Mrs. Joseph H. Hagen, New York

66 *Football [Soccer] (Study) – Football (Étude).* 1917–18 (190)
Watercolor on cardboard, 31¹/₂ × 19⁵/₈″. Private collection, Paris

67 *Third Version. The Cardiff Team – Troisième représentation. L'Équipe de Cardiff.* 1913 (124)
Oil on canvas, 128³/₈ × 81⁷/₈″. Musée du Petit Palais, Paris

68 *Football [Soccer] – Football.* 1917 (379)
Watercolor on paper, mounted on plywood, 30³/₈ × 21⁷/₈″. Private collection, Cologne

69 *Football [Soccer]. The Cardiff Team – Football. L'Équipe de Cardiff.* 1922–23 (199)
Oil on canvas, 57¹/₂ × 44¹/₂″. Collection Louis Carré, Paris

70 *Carrousel with Pigs* or *Electric Carrousel – Manège de cochons* or *Manège électrique.* 1922 (194)
Oil on canvas, 98³/₈ × 98³/₈″. Musée National d'Art Moderne, Paris

Photocredits

Bibliography

Writings by Robert Delaunay

"Über das Licht," free tr. into German by Paul Klee of "La Lumière," *Der Sturm*, III, no. 144–45, January, 1913.

"Lettre ouverte au *Sturm*," *Der Sturm*, IV, no. 194–95, January, 1914. The letter, dated December 17, 1913, refers to the article "Simultanéité futuriste" by Umberto Boccioni, which had appeared in *Der Sturm* in December, 1913 (see below, entry under "Literature").

"Entre Peintres: Lettre de Robert Delaunay," *L'Intransigeant*, March 10, 1914.

"Henri Rousseau le Douanier," *L'Amour de l'art*, no. 7, November, 1920.

"Réponse à enquête: Chez les Cubistes," *Le Bulletin de la vie artistique*, V, no. 21, November 1, 1924.

"Art abstrait et peinture vraie: Un Texte inédit de Robert Delaunay," ed. by Pierre Francastel, *Prisme des arts*, no. 2, 1956.

"Un Texte inédit de Robert Delaunay," *Aujourd'hui*, no. 11, January, 1957.

Du Cubisme à l'art abstrait, previously unpublished writings, ed. by Pierre Francastel and followed with a catalog of Robert Delaunay's work by Guy Habasque, Paris, 1957 (see below, comment under "Literature").

For further Delaunay texts, see:

"Manifeste dimensionniste," loosely inserted in *Plastique*, no. 2, 1937.
Art concret, catalog of an exhibition at the Galerie R. Drouin, Paris, 1945.
"Pour ou Contre l'Art abstrait," *Amis de l'art*, no. 11, 1947.

Works containing further Delaunay texts are indicated in the following list by an asterisk (*). Some previously unpublished material is presented by Gustav Vriesen in the present book.

Literature

Monographs and articles about Delaunay as well as works with important references are presented seriatim by year, with periodicals listed first, catalogs next, and books last. When not chronological, the order is alphabetical. The list depends essentially on information in (1) Delaunay, *Du Cubisme à l'art abstrait*, cited above; (2) Jean Cassou, preface to the catalog of the Robert Delaunay exhibition, Musée National d'Art Moderne, Paris, 1957; (3) René Jullian, "Les Delaunay," preface to the catalog of the Robert and Sonia Delaunay exhibition, Musée de Lyon, 1959; and (4) Hans Platte, preface to the catalog of the Robert Delaunay exhibition, Kunstverein, Hamburg; Wallraf-Richartz Museum, Cologne; and Kunstverein, Frankfurt, 1962 (all titles are listed again below).

Undated Works

BODMER, H. BING, *Camille Bombois*, Paris.

COQUIOT, GUSTAVE, *Les Indépendants (1884–1920)*, Paris.

GIROU, JEAN, *Peintres du Midi*, Paris.

GLEIZES, ALBERT, unpublished manuscript on Robert Delaunay; cited in Delaunay, *Du Cubisme à l'art abstrait*, Bibliography.

1910

METZINGER, JEAN, "Note sur la peinture," *Pan*, III, no. 10, 1910.

1911

APOLLINAIRE, GUILLAUME, "Les Indépendants," *L'Intransigeant*, April 20, 1911.

——, "Le Salon des Indépendants," *L'Intransigeant*, April 21, 1911.

ALLARD, ROGER, "Sur Quelques Peintres," *Les Marches du sud-ouest*, no. 2, June, 1911.

1912

ALLARD, ROGER, "Mlle Marie Laurencin. Robert Delaunay," *La Cote*, February 28, 1912.

APOLLINAIRE, GUILLAUME, "Marie Laurencin, Robert Delaunay," *L'Intransigeant*, March, 5, 1912.

——, "Le Salon des Indépendants," *L'Intransigeant*, March 19, 1912.

ALLARD, ROGER, "Le Salon des Artistes Indépendants," *La Cote*, March 20, 1912.

KLEE, PAUL, "Die Ausstellung des 'Modernen Bundes' im Kunsthaus Zürich," *Die Alpen* (Bern), VI, no. 12, August, 1912.

APOLLINAIRE, GUILLAUME, "Les Commencements du Cubisme," *Le Temps*, October 14, 1912.

* ——, "Réalité: Peinture pure," *Les Soirées de Paris*, no. 11, 1912; reprinted in *Der Sturm*, III, no. 138–39, December, 1912. See also Guillaume Apollinaire, *Il y a*, Paris, 1925, 1949.

PRINCET, MAURICE, "Robert Delaunay," preface to *R. Delaunay – M. Laurencin*, catalog of the exhibition, Galerie Barbazanges, Paris, 1912.

BUSSE, ERWIN VON, "Die Kompositionsmittel bei Robert Delaunay," *Der Blaue Reiter*, Munich, 1912.

SALMON, ANDRÉ, *La Jeune Peinture française*, Société des Trente, Paris, 1912.

1913

La Palette (ANDRÉ SALMON), "L'Art français en Allemagne," *Gil Blas*, January, 28, 1913.

APOLLINAIRE, GUILLAUME, "Die moderne Malerei," tr. of "La Peinture moderne," *Der Sturm*, III, no. 148–49, February, 1913.

BOMMERSHEIM, PAUL, "Die Überwindung der Perspektive und Robert Delaunay," *Der Sturm*, III, no. 148–49, February, 1913.

"French Artist at Odds with N. Y. Exhibitors," *The New York Tribune*, March 2, 1913.

"Mémento de la vie à Paris," *Montjoie!*, I, no. 3, March 14, 1913.

APOLLINAIRE, GUILLAUME, "Le Salon des Indépendants," *L'Intransigeant*, March 18, 1913.

——, "À Travers le Salon des Indépendants," *Montjoie!*, I, supplement to no. 13, March 18, 1913.

WARNOD, ANDRÉ, "Le Salon des Indépendants: I. Fauves et Cubistes," *Comoedia*, March 18, 1913.

APOLLINAIRE, GUILLAUME, "Le Salon des Indépendants," *L'Intransigeant*, March 25, 1913.

"Aux Indépendants," *Gil Blas*, March 26, 1913.

"Le Salon des Indépendants," *La Cote*, March 31, 1913.

HAUSENSTEIN, WILHELM, "Vom Kubismus," *Der Sturm*, IV, no. 170–71, July, 1913.

"Chronique mensuelle," *Les Soirées de Paris*, no. 18, November 15, 1913.

BEHNE, ADOLF, "Der Berliner Herbstsalon," *Die neue Kunst*, December, 1913.

BOCCIONI, UMBERTO, "Simultanéité futuriste," *Der Sturm*, IV, no. 190–91, December, 1913.

APOLLINAIRE, GUILLAUME, *Robert Delaunay*, album with eleven plates, a catalog, and a preface, published on the occasion of the Delaunay exhibition at *Der Sturm's* gallery, 1913 (Berlin, 1913).

——, *Méditations esthétiques: Les Peintres cubistes*, Paris, 1913. English eds., New York, 1944, 1949. German ed., Geneva, 1950.

1914

APOLLINAIRE, GUILLAUME, "Les Réformations du costume," *Le Mercure de France*, January 1, 1914; reprinted in Guillaume Apollinaire, *Anecdotiques*, Paris, 1955.

SALMON, ANDRÉ, "Le Salon," *Montjoie!*, special issue on the Thirtieth Salon des Indépendants, March, 1914.

HELSEY, ÉDOUARD, "En Toute Indépendance au Salon des Indépendants," *Le Journal*, March 2, 1914.

APOLLINAIRE, GUILLAUME, "Au Salon des Indépendants," *L'Intransigeant*, March 4, 1914.

WARNOD, ANDRÉ, "Petites Nouvelles des lettres et des arts: Critiques?" *Comoedia*, March 7, 1914.

CRAVAN, ARTHUR, "L'Exposition des Indépendants," *Maintenant*, special issue, March–April, 1914.

VROMANT, MARC, "À Propos du Salon des Indépendants: Du Cubisme et autres synthèses," *Comoedia*, April 15, 1914.

——, "La Peinture simultaniste: À Propos d'une étude de M. Smirnoff," *Comoedia*, June 2, 1914.

APOLLINAIRE, GUILLAUME, "Simultanisme – Librettisme," *Les Soirées de Paris*, no. 25, June 15, 1914.

"Chroniques mensuelles: Peintres allemands," *Les Soirées de Paris*, no. 25, June 15, 1914.

1915

WRIGHT, WILLARD HUNTINGTON, *Modern Painting: Its Tendency and Meaning*, New York, 1915.

1917

* "El Simultanisme del Senyor y de la Senyora Delaunay," *Vell i Nou* (Barcelona), II, no. 57, December 15, 1917.

SACS, JOÀN, *La Pintura Francesa Moderna fins al Cubisme*, Publicaciones de *La Revista*, Barcelona, 1917.

1918

GÓMEZ DE LA SERNA, RAMÓN, "El Simultanismo," *El Fígaro* (Madrid), October 23, 1918.

1919

CENDRARS, BLAISE, "Le 'Cube' s'effrite," *La Rose rouge*, May 15, 1919· reprinted in Blaise Cendrars, *Aujourd'hui*, Paris, 1931.

——, "Delaunay: Le Contraste simultané," *La Rose rouge*, July 24, 1919; reprinted in Blaise Cendrars, *Aujourd'hui*, Paris, 1931.

LANDSBERGER, FRANZ, *Impressionismus und Expressionismus: Eine Einführung in das Wesen der neuen Kunst*, Leipzig, 1919.

1920

GÓMEZ DE LA SERNA, RAMÓN, "Los Delaunays," *El Pombo* (Madrid), 1920.

KÜPPERS, PAUL E., *Der Kubismus*, Leipzig, 1920.

1921

GEORGE, WALDEMAR, "Robert Delaunay et le triomphe de la couleur," *La Vie des lettres et des arts*, no. 11, 1921.

SALMON, ANDRÉ, "L'Orphisme," *Action*, April, 1921.

1922

ARAGON, LOUIS, "Delaunay," *Littérature*, n.s. 4, September 1, 1922.

SALMON, ANDRÉ, *Propos d'atelier*, Paris, 1922, 1938.

1923

SOUPAULT, PHILIPPE, "Robert Delaunay, peintre," *Feuilles libres*, no. 33, September–October, 1923.

——, "Robert Delaunay," *Het Overzicht* (Antwerp), no. 18–19, October, 1923.

1924

* GOLL, IVAN (GOLLIVAN), "Le Peintre Robert Delaunay parle," *Surréalisme*, no. 1, October, 1924.

* FELS, FLORENT, "Propos d'artistes: Robert Delaunay," *Nouvelles littéraires*, October 25, 1924.

CHENEY, SHELDON, *A Primer of Modern Art*, New York, 1924.

HILDEBRANDT, HANS, *Die Kunst des XIX. und XX. Jahrhunderts: Handbuch der Kunstwissenschaft*, Potsdam, 1924.

1925

DELTEIL, JOSEPH, "Robert Delaunay, peintre de jour," *Les Arts plastiques*, no. 1, March, 1925.

VORONCA, ILARIE, "Simultaneismul in Arta," *Integral* (Bucharest), no. 6–7, 1925.

* LISSITZKY, EL and ARP, HANS, *Die Kunstismen*, Zurich, 1925.

OZENFANT, AMÉDÉE, and JEANNERET, C. E. (LE CORBUSIER), *La Peinture moderne*, Paris, 1925.

1926

CHÉRONNET, LOUIS, "Publicité moderne: Fernand Léger et Robert Delaunay," *L'Art vivant*, December 1, 1926.

GEORGE, WALDEMAR, "Lithographies de R. Delaunay," *L'Amour de l'art*, no. 7, 1926.

GOLL, CLAIRE, "Der Delaunay-Stil," *Börsen-Kurier* (Berlin), 1926.

APOLLINAIRE, GUILLAUME, *Anecdotiques*, Paris, 1926, 1955.

CENDRARS, BLAISE, *Profond aujourd'hui*, Paris, 1926.

EINSTEIN, CARL, *Die Kunst des 20. Jahrhunderts*, vol. 16 of *Propyläen-Kunstgeschichte*, Berlin, 1926.

1927

* RAYNAL, MAURICE, *Anthologie de la peinture en France de 1906 à nos jours*, Paris, 1927.

1928

GLEIZES, ALBERT, *Kubismus* (Bauhausbücher no. 13), Munich, 1928.
OZENFANT, AMÉDÉE, *Art*, Paris, 1928.
UHDE, WILHELM, *Picasso et la tradition française*, Paris, 1928.

1929

GLEIZES, ALBERT, "L'Épopée: De la Forme immobile à la forme mobile," *Le Rouge et le noir*, special issue on the arts, June–July, 1929.
JANNEAU, GUILLAUME, *L'Art cubiste: Théories et réalisations, étude critique*, Paris, 1929.

1930

FELS, FLORENT, "Robert Delaunay," *Vu*, October 1, 1930.

1931

HIDALGO, ALBERTO, "Robert Delaunay, el didactor," *El Hogar* (Buenos Aires), March 27, 1931; reprinted in Alberto Hidalgo, *Diario di mi Sentimiento*, Buenos Aires, 1937.
OZENFANT, AMÉDÉE, *Foundations of Modern Art*, New York, 1931, 1952.
——, *Leben und Gestaltung*, Potsdam, 1931.

1933

COLOMBIER, PIERRE DU, and MANUEL, ROLAND, *Tableau du XXe siècle, 1900–1933: Les Arts, la musique et la danse*, Paris, 1933.
HAMANN, RICHARD, *Geschichte der Kunst*, Berlin, 1933; numerous later eds.
READ, HERBERT, *Art Now: An Introduction to the Theory of Modern Painting and Sculpture*, London, 1933, 1934; rev. ed., 1936; rev. and enl. ed., 1948, 1950.
STEIN, GERTRUDE, *The Autobiography of Alice B. Toklas*, New York, 1933; later eds. French ed., Paris, 1934. German ed., Zurich, 1955.

1934

BAZIN, GERMAIN, "L'Orphisme," *L'Amour de l'art*, special issue, "Histoire de l'art contemporain," ed. by René Huyghe, 1934; reprinted in René Huyghe, *Histoire de l'art contemporain – La Peinture*, Paris, 1935.
LHOTE, ANDRÉ, "Naissance du Cubisme," *L'Amour de l'art*, special issue, "Histoire de l'art contemporain," ed. by René Huyghe, 1934; reprinted in René Huyghe, *Histoire de l'art contemporain – La Peinture*, Paris, 1935.
BESSON, GEORGES, *La Peinture française au XXe siècle*, Paris, 1934.

1935

CASSOU, JEAN, "R. Delaunay et la plastique murale en couleur," *Art et décoration*, March, 1935.

1936

BARR, ALFRED H., JR., *Cubism and Abstract Art*, New York, 1936.

1937

"Palais de l'Aéronautique," *Les Nouvelles de l'Exposition* (Paris), III, no. 5, May 1, 1937.
MARÉCHAL, JEAN, "La Section de l'art Abstrait," *Le petit Parisien*, May 30, 1937.
GOUJON, JEAN, "Au Pavillon de l'Air," *L'Intransigeant*, June 25, 1937.
LOT, FERNAND, "Une Grande Orchestration de l'art abstrait," *Marianne*, July 7, 1937.
CHÉRONNET, LOUIS, "L'Homme et ses transports," *Marianne*, August 18, 1937.
ESCHOLIER, RAYMOND, *La Peinture française: XXe siècle*, Paris, 1937.
REBAY, HILLA, *Innovation: Une Nouvelle Ère artistique*, Paris, 1937.

1938

DEFRIES, AMELIA, *Purpose in Design*, London, 1938.
GILLES DE LA TOURETTE, F., *La Peinture française contemporaine*, Paris, n.d. (1938).
ZERVOS, CHRISTIAN, *Histoire de l'art contemporain*, Paris, 1938.

1939

TERRASSE, CHARLES, *La Peinture française au XXe siècle*, Paris, 1939.

1940

A. E. Gallatin Collection: "Museum of Living Art," Philadelphia, Philadelphia Museum of Art, 1940; rev. ed., 1958.

1942

* GUGGENHEIM, PEGGY, *Art of This Century*, catalog of collection objects, New York, 1942.

1943

AEGERTER, EMMANUEL, and LABRACHERIE, PIERRE, *Guillaume Apollinaire*, Paris, 1943.

1944

DORIVAL, BERNARD, *Le Fauvisme et le Cubisme: 1905–1911*, vol. 2 of *Les Étapes de la peinture française contemporaine*, Paris, 1944.

1945

BONFANTE, EGIDIO, and RAVENNA, JUTI, *Arte cubista*, Venice, 1945.
DIEHL, GASTON (ed.), *Les Problèmes de la peinture*, Paris, 1945.
HUYGHE, RENÉ, *La Peinture actuelle: La Peinture française*, Paris, 1945.
VIARD, PAUL, *L'Âme de Robert Delaunay*, Paris, 1945.

1946

GIEDION-WELCKER, CAROLA, "R. Delaunay," *Das Werk* (Winterthur), no. 8, 1946.
CASSOU, JEAN, "Robert Delaunay," preface to the catalog of the Robert Delaunay exhibition, Galerie Louis Carré, Paris, 1946.

1947

DAVIS, RICHARD S., "Institute Acquires Cubist Masterpiece," *Bulletin of the Minneapolis Institute of Arts*, XXXVI, 1947.
LASSAIGNE, JACQUES, *Cent Chefs-d'œuvre des peintres de l'École de Paris*, Paris, 1947.
——, COGNIAT, RAYMOND, and ZARAH, MARCEL, *Panorama des arts*, Paris, 1947.
RAYNAL, MAURICE, *Peintres du XXe siècle*, Geneva, 1947.

1949

ARP, HANS, *Onze Peintres vus par Arp*, Zurich, 1949.
* DELTEIL, JOSEPH, "R. Delaunay," in Michel Seuphor, *L'Art abstrait: Ses Origines, ses premiers maîtres*, Paris, 1949, 1950.
* HABASQUE, GUY, "La Technique de Robert Delaunay," in Michel Seuphor, *L'Art abstrait: Ses Origines, ses premiers maîtres*, Paris, 1949, 1950.
HUYGHE, RENÉ, *Les Contemporains*, Paris, 1949.
SAN LAZZARO, GUALTIERI DI, *Painting in France, 1895–1949*, London, 1949.

1950

SEUPHOR, MICHEL, "L'Orphisme," *Art d'aujourd'hui*, March, 1950.
FELS, FLORENT, *L'Art vivant de 1900 à nos jours*, Geneva, 1950.
GILLES DE LA TOURETTE, F., *Robert Delaunay*, Paris, 1950.
RAYNAL, MAURICE, *De Picasso au Surréalisme*, vol. 3 of *Histoire de la*

peinture moderne, Geneva, 1950. English ed., *From P casso to Surrea sm*, vol. 3 of *Modern Pa.nting*, Geneva, 1950.

SCHMIDT, GEORG, "Franz Marc und August Macke im Kreise ihrer Zeitgenossen," *appendix to Jahresbericht der öf,entlichen Kunstsammlungen Basel, 1946–1950*, Basel, 1950.

1951

CASSOU, JEAN, "R. Delaunay," *Kunst und Volk* (Zurich), July, 1951.

DEGAND, LÉON, "Robert Delaunay," *Art d'aujourd'hui*, no. 8, 1951.

* RÜDLINGER, A., preface to the catalog of the Robert Delaunay exhibition, Kunsthalle, Bern, 1951.

BARR, ALFRED H., JR., *Matisse: His Art and His Public*, New York, 1951.

CIRLOT, J. E., *La Pintura abstracta*, Barcelona, 1951.

FRANCASTEL, PIERRE, *Peinture et societé*, Lyons, 1951.

1952

ADÉMA, MARCEL, *Guillaume Apollinaire le mal-aimé*, Paris, 1952.

SCHMIDT, PAUL FERDINAND, *Geschichte der modernen Malerei*, Stuttgart, 1952; 9th ed., 1961.

1953

"Le Cubisme," *Art d'aujourd'hui*, May–June, 1953.

BAYÓN, D. C., "Discusión del Cubismo," *Ver y Estimar* (Buenos Aires), IX, December, 1953.

HEATH, ADRIAN, *Abstract Painting, Its Origin and Meaning*, London, 1953.

HESS, WALTER, *Das Problem der Farbe in den Selbstzeugnissen moderner Maler*, Munich, 1953.

* VRIESEN, GUSTAV, *August Macke*, Stuttgart, 1953, 1957.

1954

BARR, ALFRED H., JR. (ed.), *Masters of Modern Art*, The Museum of Modern Art, New York, 1954.

GEORGES-MICHEL, MICHEL, *De Renoir à Picasso: Les Peintres que j'ai connus*, Paris, 1954.

HAFTMANN, WERNER, *Malerei im 20. Jahrhundert*, Munich, 1954, 1962. English ed., vol. 1 of *Painting in the Twentieth Century*, New York, 1960; later eds.

WALDEN, NELL, *Der Sturm, ein Gedenkbuch an Herwarth Walden und die Künstler des Sturmkreises*, Baden-Baden, 1954.

1955

BRU, CHARLES-PIERRE, *Esthétique de l'abstraction: Essai sur le problème actuel de la peinture*, Paris, 1955.

FRANCASTEL, PIERRE, *Du Classicisme au Cubisme*, vol. 2 of *Histoire de la peinture française*, Paris, 1955.

GENAILLE, ROBERT, *La Peinture contemporaine*, Paris, 1955.

HAFTMANN, WERNER, *Malerei im 20. Jahrhundert*, Munich, 1955, 1960, 1962. English ed., vol. 2 of *Painting in the Twentieth Century*, New York, 1960; later eds.

HUYGHE, RENÉ, *Dialogue avec le visible*, Paris, 1955. German ed., *Die Antwort der Bilder*, Vienna, 1958. English ed., *Idea and Image in World Art: Dialogue with the Visible*, New York, 1959.

1956

SCHWEICHER, C., preface to the catalog of the Robert Delaunay exhibition, Städtisches Museum Leverkusen (Schloss Morsbroich); Kunstverein, Freiburg im Breisgau; Kunsthalle, Mannheim, 1956.

BRION, MARCEL, *L'Abstraction*, "Tendances de la peinture moderne," Paris, 1956.

——, *Art abstrait*, Paris, 1956.

DESCARGUES, PIERRE, *Le Cubisme*, "Tendances de la peinture moderne," Paris, 1956.

HESS, WALTER, *Dokumente zum Verständnis der modernen Malerei*, Hamburg, 1956.

RAGON, MICHEL, *L'Aventure de l'art abstrait*, Paris, 1956.

1957

HENNIGER, GERD, "Paul Klee und Robert Delaunay," *Quadrum*, III, 1957.

CASSOU, JEAN, preface to the catalog of the Robert Delaunay exhibition, Musée National d'Art Moderne, Paris, 1957.

Catalogus 177: Robert Delaunay, Stedelijk Museum, Amsterdam, and Stedelijk van Abbemuseum, Eindhoven, 1957.

* IMDAHL, MAX, "Die Farbe als Licht bei August Macke," in *August Macke: Gedenkausstellung zum 70. Geburtstag*, catalog of the exhibition, Landesmuseum, Münster, 1957.

DORIVAL, BERNARD, *Nabis, Fauves, Cubistes*, vol. 1 of *Les Peintres du vingtième siècle*, Paris, 1957. English ed., *Twentieth Century Painters (French Painting)*, New York, 1958. German ed., *Die französischen Maler des 20. Jahrhunderts*, Munich, 1959.

FRANCASTEL, PIERRE, "Introduction," in Robert Delaunay, *Du Cubisme à l'art abstrait*, ed. by Pierre Francastel and followed with a catalog of Robert Delaunay's work by Guy Habasque, Paris, 1957.

HOFMANN, WERNER, *Zeichen und Gestalt: Die Malerei des 20. Jahrhunderts*, Frankfurt am Main, 1957.

MYERS, BERNARD S., *The German Expressionists: A Generation in Revolt*, New York, 1957. German ed., Cologne, 1957.

PLATTE, HANS, *Die Kunst des 20. Jahrhunderts: Malerei*, Munich, 1957.

1958

* CHIPP, H. B., "Orphism and Color Theory," *The Art Bulletin*, XL, 1958.

PLATTE, HANS, "Robert Delaunay und Lyonel Feininger," in *Jahrbuch der Hamburger Kunstsammlungen*, III, Hamburg, 1958.

ZAHN, LEOPOLD, *Eine Geschichte der modernen Kunst*, Berlin, 1958.

1959

JULLIAN, RENÉ, "Les Delaunay," preface to the catalog of the Robert and Sonia Delaunay exhibition, Musée de Lyon, 1959.

SEUPHOR, MICHEL, "The Idea of Construction – Notes and Reflections," preface to *Construction and Geometry in Painting: From Malewitch to Tomorrow*, catalog of an exhibition, Galerie Chalette, New York, 1959.

BUCHHEIM, LOTHAR-GÜNTHER, *Der Blaue Reiter*, Feldafing, 1959.

GOLDING, JOHN, *Cubism: A History and an Analysis, 1907–1914*, London, 1959.

HABASQUE, GUY, *Cubism*, Geneva, 1959.

SEUPHOR, MICHEL, *La Sculpture de ce siècle*, Neuchâtel, 1959. English ed., *The Sculpture of This Century*, New York, 1960.

1960

FRANCASTEL, PIERRE, "Les Delaunay," *XXᵉ Siècle*, XXII, no. 15, 1960.

HAMM, H., "Robert Delaunay und der kubistische Stil," *Die Kunst und das schöne Heim*, LVIII, 1960.

BRION, MARCEL, *Geschichte der abstrakten Kunst*, Cologne, 1960, 1961.

CASSOU, JEAN, *Panorama des arts plastiques contemporains*, Paris, 1960.

ROSENBLUM, ROBERT, *Cubism and Twentieth Century Art*, New York, 1960, 1966. German ed., Stuttgart, 1960.

1961

REVEL, JEAN-FRANÇOIS, "Le Cubisme mis en regard de l'art abstrait," *Connaissance des arts*, February, 1961.

STENEBERG, EDUARD, "Robert Delaunay und die deutsche Malerei," *Das Kunstwerk*, October, 1961.

SOURIAU, ÉTIENNE, "Y-a-t'il une Palette française?" *Arts de France*, II, 1962.

* PLATTE, HANS, preface to the catalog of the Robert Delaunay exhibition, Kunstverein, Hamburg; Wallraf-Richartz Museum, Cologne; and Kunstverein, Frankfurt, 1962.

BERGMAN, P., *Modernolatria et Simultaneità*, Uppsala, 1962.

LANGNER, JOHANNES, "Zu den Fenster-Bildern von Robert Delaunay," in *Jahrbuch der Hamburger Kunstsammlungen*, VII, Hamburg, 1962.

1963

DORIVAL, BERNARD, "La Donation Delaunay au Musée National d'Art Moderne," *La Revue du Louvre*, XIII, no. 6, 1963.

RAPPAPORT, RUTHANN, "Robert Delaunay and Cubism, 1909–1913," unpublished master's dissertation, New York University, 1963.

1964

MEYER, FRANZ, "Robert Delaunay, 'Hommage à Blériot, 1914,'" in *Jahresbericht 1962 der öffentlichen Kunstsammlung Basel*, Basel, 1964.

SCHMIDT, GEORG, *Robert Delaunay*, Baden-Baden, 1964.

1965

SCHMALENBACH, WERNER, introduction to *Katalog der Kunstsammlung Nordrhein-Westfalen*, Düsseldorf, 1965.

BIRREN, FABER, *History of Color in Painting, with New Principles of Color Expression*, New York, 1965.

SCHMALENBACH, WERNER, "Robert Delaunay: *Eiffelturm* (Museum Folkwang)," in *Das Meisterwerk: Kunstbetrachtungen in Einzelinterpretationen*, Recklinghausen, 1965, vol. 3.

1966

* IMDAHL, MAX, "Die Rolle der Farbe in der neueren französischen Malerei: Abstraktion und Konkretion," in *Hermeneutik, Immanente Ästhetik – Ästhetische Reflexion*, vol. 2 of *Poetik und Hermeneutik*, Munich, 1966.

——, "Probleme der Optical Art," *Kunstchronik*, XIX, October, 1966.

1967

* IMDAHL, MAX, "Probleme der Optical Art," *Wallraf-Richartz-Jahrbuch*, XXIX, 1967.